# Teaching Athletics
## 8 – 13

# Teaching Athletics 8 – 13

## Guidelines for the non-specialist

David A. Evans

HODDER AND STOUGHTON
LONDON  SYDNEY  AUCKLAND  TORONTO

British Library Cataloguing in Publication Data

Evans, David A.
  Teaching athletics 8–13.
  1. Track-athletics–Coaching
  I. Title
  796.4'2'07      GV1060.5

ISBN 0 340 34712 0

First published 1984

Photoset in 11/12 Plantin (CRTronic) by Multiplex Medway Ltd.

Printed and bound in Great Britain for
Hodder and Stoughton Educational, .
a division of Hodder and Stoughton Ltd,
Mill Road, Dunton Green, Sevenoaks, Kent,
by Biddles Ltd., Guildford and King's Lynn.

# Contents

# Acknowledgments

I am grateful to a number of people for their assistance with this book: Bob Sussex for invaluable advice and encouragement in the formative stages; Maureen O'Neill and Rena Taylor for transforming my erratic scrawl into excellent typescript; Robin Nicholls and Duncan Harris for their photographs; the many club and school athletes who provided the raw material from which my ideas have developed.

1983                                                                 D.A.E.

This book is dedicated to the multitude of athletes who, to paraphrase Charles Hamilton Sorley, 'do not run for prize ...' but run because they must through the great wide air ... who run because they like it through the broad bright land.

# Preface

Most books on athletics are written for those coaching adult, male athletes. A few are aimed at the younger age groups, and even fewer are aimed at *teaching* large groups in a club or school situation and containing a wide range of ability. Even these few books are written for secondary schools which have Physical Education (P.E.) Departments with several specialist physical education teachers.

This is not intended as a coaching manual with detailed description of skills but is more concerned with the approach to and organisation of athletics for young children, for it is believed that, if these two aspects are right, then the enthusiasm for learning skills and participating in athletics will follow. This is not to say that skills teaching is unimportant. It is very important, and the 'skill hungry' years of eight to 13 are the right time to teach skills, but many teachers are wary of teaching athletics because they do not feel they have sufficient knowledge of advanced skills. It is hoped that this book will give a sufficient explanation of the basic skills in athletics to enable these to be taught and thus form a sound base on which later teaching/coaching can build. Teachers wishing to gain greater knowledge of athletics should refer to the bibliography at the back of the book.

In most junior and middle schools, even those where a P.E. specialist is on the staff, all members of the staff will take some P.E. This book is designed to be of use to all teachers, including the P.E. specialist, who wish to teach athletics as a purposeful activity and part of a full physical education programme in their schools. Athletics is, or should be, for all children, not for just a selected few, and properly presented can provide a purposeful and enjoyable activity throughout the summer term, if not the whole year. The main problem will be coping with over-enthusiasm. May it always be so.

Many of the suggested conditioning games and activities may also be of use to those involved in coaching large groups in the eight to 13 age range at club level.

# Introduction

Athletics can play three inter-related roles in a school. It has a value for all other forms of physical education, it can link with most aspects of the curriculum, and it can provide for all children.

First, it has a strong link with all other forms of physical education, because the fitter, faster and stronger the children are then the better will be their performance in any sporting activity. Whatever the level of initial skill children possess, as they tire the level of skill fades. Fit footballers or netball players, for example, will be able to perform their skills at a greater speed and over a longer period of time. The physical education programme in a school should aim at giving children a broad base of skills in a range of sports. The wide range of skills that come in running, jumping and throwing in athletics, together with the even wider range in the conditioning activities, make athletics an invaluable part of the physical education programme.

Secondly, athletics can add a new dimension to the academic curriculum, as it can easily be related to most subjects and so serve as an excellent stimulus. For example, mathematics can be stimulated by the measuring of jumping activities. It is far more interesting to measure standing long jumps than the school hall (again). The measurements recorded can then be used for simple addition, comparison, modes, means, medians and graphs. Timing can lead to work on metres per second, combined with the previous activities. In language work, not only factual writing on athletics events or lessons, but also creative writing of prose and poetry on the sensations of running and jumping and competing, spring readily to mind. By utilising major athletics events such as Olympic, European or Commonwealth Games, European or World Cup events, various aspects of Geography, History or topic work can be linked. The effect of exercise on breathing and pulse beat, the use of limbs, muscles and levers, can enhance simple human biology. (See Appendix II, pages 114–15.) Furthermore, academically weak children, who can notice their improvement in an athletics event through personal effort, may transfer that effort and confidence into classroom work, particularly if the starting-point is a sport in which they have achieved some success.

Thirdly, and most important, athletics is an enjoyable and beneficial activity that can provide for all children. It embraces a number of different activities and usually children can find one which is appropriate to their physique. Many points can be made to support this aim; some would give more weight to one than to others but the order is irrelevant. They are all valid.

1  Children enjoy running, jumping and throwing. These are natural activities which they will perform without instruction. A very young child will throw toys from a pram and will ignore all attempts to correct his or her style. A child's first running steps come as a natural progression from walking, quite often without ever having seen anyone else running, and on seeing a long-jump pit most children need no urging to run and jump into the sand. It is logical, therefore, that we should channel this innate urge into purposeful activity and help children to improve their performance so they may measure their success.

> Healthy children vie with each other in many informal games to find out who runs fastest, jumps highest or throws furthest. In this sense they can be described as natural athletes.
> *Movement: Physical Education in the Primary Years*
>           (Department of Education and Science, 1972)

2  There is no direct opposition – no one is trying to prevent children from performing at their best, no one tackles them or places a ball out of reach or at high speed. If properly taught, children can measure their success against their own previous efforts.

3  Progress (that is, success) in athletics can be measured and take place at a suitable pace. For children of limited ability this is particularly satisfying, because they can see their improvement and are not frustrated by the introduction of a new set of skills as soon as they master one set. The talented child has unlimited targets and is not restricted by any lack of ability on the part of other children in the class. Progress can be

recorded in terms of improvement as well as personal bests –
for example, a 3.2 metre long jump could also be recorded as
+ 35 centimetres, indicating a 35 centimetre improvement.

4  The basic rules of athletics are simple and easy to understand and, although basic skills should be taught, lack of skill
does not prevent children from completing their activity. A
stuttering, uncoordinated 2-metre long jump can still be
measured. The greater emphasis on the activity rather than on
the precise skill, particularly in the early stages, makes athletics far easier to teach than many teachers realise.

5  As the basic rules are straightforward, children can act as
judges. Not only is this useful to the teacher but it is also a
valuable part of a child's education in the acceptance of
responsibility. To judge in most sports is difficult for adults,
let alone for children. Decisions have to be made instantly on
fast moving actions, with several points to watch for. In athletics, a judge knows precisely when a decision has to be made
(for example, the take-off in a long jump) and it is easier to
concentrate on the one point than to look for a range of possible offences in football or netball. Mistakes will occur. Without them, little learning will take place, but the ability to measure accurately and to record information may be of greater
value later in life to most children than the performance of a
well-executed long jump. Mercifully, athletics is still free from
the almost conditioned reflex objection to any unfavourable
decision that bedevils many other sports. This too makes it
easier for a child to act as a judge in athletics as, even in small-
side games, the 'professional objector' can make refereeing
very hard for a young child.

6  Not only the physically mature, talented and confident
child who succeeds at all sports can participate in athletics, but
also the timid, the undersized, the overweight, or even the
uncoordinated child can find some pleasure and success in
some athletics event. A timid child, who is apprehensive of
being vigorously tackled or struck by a ball, may find running
rewarding, often producing the determination and courage to
keep running when tired – and that is success. Which takes
greater courage, to go fearlessly but instantly into a tackle, or
to keep running for several minutes when tired?
In all athletics events the lack of direct opposition and

removal of the fear of letting the team down is an encouragement to the timid child, and many have developed self-
confidence through athletics and transferred it to contact and
other team sports. Overweight children can find their excess
weight is an advantage in throwing events; perhaps they may
not be the best, but, for once, they are not the worst – and that
is success. Undersized or uncoordinated children can derive
satisfaction from a full-out effort without a dropped pass, a
miskick, or a tackle to spoil their endeavour. The task or
course can be completed – and that is success. Even those
medically excused P.E. (short- or long-term) can be used as
judges and thus usefully involved.

The above points are not intended to imply that athletics is
a preferable alternative to team games (especially small-side
games), which do have an important part to play alongside
gymnastics, swimming, movement and so on in a school P.E.
curriculum. The points are made to ensure the inclusion of
athletics in a balanced P.E. timetable.

Athletics is fun and children will gain pleasure and satisfaction out of performing simple skills and measuring their
improvement. This alone might be sufficient justification for
including athletics in the P.E. curriculum, but, in addition to
learning physical skills, children will improve their ability in
timing, measuring and recording; they will learn to take
responsibility; and they will learn that improvement comes
with practice and effort. They should also learn that winning
is not everything, nor is losing the end of the world, and certainly the honour of the school does not depend on victory on
the sports field, though it may depend on how they conduct
themselves on it.

If we lose it matters not for there the sadness ends,
For defeat n'er counted as a loss, if it be the gain of friends.
*Max Boyce*

# SECTION I

## The Events

### A RUNNING

Running may take the form of sprinting, sprint relays, jogging, middle-distance and cross-country (steady pace) running, and hurdling. Each is related to the others and at times inseparable from them, and many conditioning activities for one aspect of running are also useful for others. None is harmful.

### Safety

1 If *lanes* are used, insist on children staying in lane and, at the end, coasting to a stop in a straight line, with no cutting across.

2 *Middle-distance races*. At the start do not have too many competitors so that pushing and shoving is likely, and if the start is on a bend instruct children not to cut to the inside unless they are clear.

3 *Hurdles*. Children should never attempt to jump hurdles in the wrong direction, – that is from the side away from the balance feet of the hurdle.

4 *Cross-country/fun runs*. Ensure that all gateways are clear and wide enough to prevent pushing and jostling.

5 *Listening*. As with all P.E. activities, when giving instructions insist that children are quiet, still and preferably seated or squatting down. Then they may listen.

6 If *spikes* are worn, INSIST that there shall be no running about or jumping. All children must be carefully instructed not to wear spiked shoes on wood, concrete, or tarmac. Even

more important, they should only put them on just before racing and remove them immediately afterwards. This reduces the danger of excited children forgetting they are wearing spikes and spiking another child. Also instruct children to coast to a stop and not to shuffle their feet in order to brake.

# (i) Sprinting

## The Start/Commands

It is advisable to use the correct commands from an early age, breaking away from 'Ready-Steady-Go'. This will avoid confusion and add status to the practice. In this, at least, children are emulating Olympic stars.

Before any commands are given, all runners should stand 4–5 metres back from the starting line. When all are present, give the command '*On your marks*', whereupon they should move up to the line (see page 7 for positioning of feet). Stress that the indication that children are ready is a position of stillness and looking ahead. The starter should not give the next command while any runner is fidgeting or looking around. There is no stipulated time between the command 'On your marks' and the next command '*Set*', and it is worth deliberately varying the time lag, even holding children for a few seconds after they are ready, to make them aware of this. After 'Set' there should be a short time lag of approximately two seconds, but the starting signal (gun, whistle, clap or '*Go*') should not be given if any runner is not set (wavering). If all are not set within 3–4 seconds, say '*Stand up*', then '*Step back from the line*'. The procedure from 'On your marks' should then be repeated. With very young children, a slightly shorter gap between 'Set' and 'Go' may be used, but it must never be so short that children are not able to be set nor so long that they anticipate a short gap.

### False Starts

If one or more children go before the signal, recall them by a second shot of the gun or blast on a whistle, having previously explained which will be used and why. A whistle is ideal, being cheaper than a gun (2p a shot for a .22) and louder than a voice, but it is not too satisfactory as a starting implement as, ideally, the starter should be standing to the side of the athletes and slightly in front. Thus children see the intake of breath before blowing the whistle. A toy cap gun can be effective and many coaches at club level use them for practices.

*Curing false starts*
The remedy lies in the practices. Athletes who have been well taught and disciplined in practice are much less likely to make a false start in competition, although nerves and a different starter may still combine to produce some false starts. In practices, be strict on false starts. One effective disciplinary measure is to move offenders back one metre for each false start.

Disqualification in practice is not very effective, but being moved back a metre at a time carries a clear message to persistent offenders.

## Starting technique

### 1 *Crouch start*
For a young child in plimsolls or trainers, a crouch start is likely to be more of a handicap than a help. Without spikes, the back foot is much more likely to slip, especially on shiny or damp grass or cinders. Secondly, even with spikes, the correct position demands a shoulder and arm strength few will possess. Finally, most young children, even at secondary level, when performing a crouch start stand up on 'Go' and then move forward. They might as well have been standing to begin with. Much more important than imposing a difficult skill on youngsters, one which only a few will master, is teaching a positive, quick reaction to the starting signal. A slip at the start is disastrous, and a poorly executed crouch start is inferior to the standing start which is strongly recommended for young children.

### 2 *Standing start*
**On your marks**
(a) Front toe to line, back foot a small step behind. (Children should use whichever foot they prefer as the front foot.)
(b) Slight lean forward, looking ahead.
(c) Arms relaxed.
(d) Front knee slightly bent.

With all skills it is important to select a few *key factors*. These can never describe the whole skill, but children can only remember a few points at a time. Refinements can be added later.

1   Starts: it is important to look ahead, not at the starter. The three girls on the left have the better positions.

## Set

(a) Increase body lean. Keep looking ahead.
(b) Increase bend of front knee.
(c) Feel for ground with back foot.

The feeling for the ground not only checks over-balancing but also ensures firm contact, thus lessening the chance of slipping. No mention is made of *arms* – except to keep them relaxed. If young children are told to put their arms in a running position, most will put their left arm with their left leg and vice-versa. This is a natural position for balance, but not very effective for starting. Photographs of the start of international middle-distance races often show athletes standing with arms and legs out of synchronisation, so it is not worth spending too much time on arm positions. Avoid too exaggerated or too tense positions. Thus arms loose in front or slightly bent forward are quite acceptable.

## Go

In reality, with this age group only one word is needed – *Run* – and that is usually superfluous, although many technical hints could be given and abound in most text books, such as drive with the arms, push with the front foot, and bring the rear foot through quickly.

## Style

There are no medals for style, and usually faults in style smooth out as the young athletes get fitter.

*Avoid*  1  Wide arm swinging.

         2  Looking round or to the side.

         3  Tension – gritting teeth, clenching fists, straining the head back – this is like cycling with brakes on.

*Stress*  1  Keep in lane.

         2  Look ahead.

         3  Run tall.

         4  Run past the finishing line before slowing down to stop, keeping in a straight line (this avoids accidents and helps the judges).

## Conditioning activities for sprints

### 1 *Short races*

Several short races of 20 to 30 metres with five or six children per race are preferable to longer races with larger numbers. First, the closer the children are to the teacher, the greater the control. Secondly, more races will increase the amount of starting practice and the opportunities to give advice on style. Thirdly, fatigue is less likely.

It is not advisable to let the same children win each time – or come last. One ideal way of providing variety and incentive is a handicap race. After each race, the winner is handicapped two paces, and the child who comes second one pace. The last athlete is advanced two paces, and the next to last one pace. Unless one child is particularly fast, or slow, the races soon become very close and several children experience the thrill of winning. The star athlete is thus challenged and, in particular, learns the value of sprinting until past the finishing line and does not get into the habit of easing up before the line which often develops if winning is easy. The effect on the slow athlete can be dramatic, too. It is easy to criticise the apparent lack of effort on the part of a child trotting in last each time. This is often a device to preserve self-respect, as losing while not trying is easier to face than losing (yet again) after giving 100 per cent. This same child, finding himself in the lead 10 metres from the finish, will continue to try hard, and even if this is a result of a generous start the satisfaction gained is enormous.

A further variant is to run winners of each race together in the next round, seconds against seconds, and so on. In this way the less skilful compete in their own races, but this, although valuable when seeking to find the best runners, will still enable the star to gain too many easy victories and the very slow child to lose regularly.

## 2  Activity games
Useful conditioning may be gained from a variety of running games such as tag, chain-he, stick-in-the-mud, and similar games. They allow for a great deal of enthusiastic running, which is ideal training for young athletes, and also provide excellent warming-up activities (see Section II, Class Lessons, page 54).

## 3  Shuttle runs (Ten-Step and Five-Star events)
Runners shuttle back and forth between two lines approximately 10 metres apart. The number of repetitions may vary, as may the distance (unless part of one of the incentive schemes dealt with later), but 6 × 10 metres is just about right. Runners may compete against themselves (in timed runs), or in small groups of two or three.

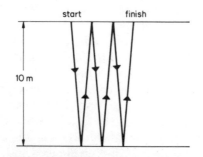

Figure 1  *Shuttle run, 6 × 10 metres*

## 4  Slalom races (Ten-Step)
Unless part of the incentive scheme this, too, can be varied. Several cones or skittles placed one metre apart provide a testing course for agility and speed; if farther apart, say 2–3 metres, there is a greater test of speed. Runners zig-zag to the end and back. This can be a time trial, or, if two or more identical courses are set up, it can be a race which can be timed if required.

finish
start

cones 1 metre apart

Figure 2  *Slalom (or Zig-zag) race*

A popular team relay, using children instead of cones, is this. Teams of six to ten children are spaced out in a hall, playground, or field. The space available dictates the numbers and spacing. The last person in line starts for each team, zig-zagging to the front, then sprints to the rear of the team (preferably round a marker) and touches number 2. Each runner zig-zags in turn to the front, sprints to the back and zig-zags back to his or her place. The last runner (the front child) starts by sprinting to the back, then zig-zagging to the front.

## 5  *Object pick-up race* (Ten-Step)
Five or six bean bags or other objects (e.g. knotted skipping ropes) are spaced out over 10–15 metres. Runners retrieve them one at a time and return them to the start. This can become a team race – number 1 picks up, 2 replaces, 3 picks up, and so on.

Outdoors, a variant using two or three footballs or rugby balls spread over a greater distance of 20–30 metres is also popular.

## 6  *Relays*
Children soon get tired of straight races but perk up at the word relays.

(a) **Shuttle relays** – a development of shuttle runs. Across a space 20–30 metres wide, two teams of children stand facing one another. Members of each team should form up in line one behind the other, even numbers one side of the open space, odd numbers the other. Athlete number 1 runs across to touch 2 (to avoid confusion, insist on all touches being right hand to right hand), who sprints back to 3, and so on. If teams are unequal in number, number 1 can run twice (the second time being when the last runner gets back to him/her). If the race is repeated, handicap a team that wins easily, or give a start to the losing team.

(b) **Pairs race.** The first runner runs 20–40 metres, touches number 2 who runs 20–40 metres to finish. If touch is right hand to left hand, this is an early activity for baton changing.

(c) **Round the track/football pitch** in teams of four. Each runner runs a quarter of the distance. If using a football pitch,
start and finish at the half-way line to avoid changes on the
corners. Although the absence of lanes may cause some confusion, each runner will sprint hard. Change-overs by touch as
in (b).

## 7  *Reaction games*

(a) **Starts over 10 metres.** Commands are simply '*Ready*' and
'*Go*'. The gap between the two should vary. For further variety the starts can be from sitting position, lying on face, on
back, head to start line, feet to start line, standing with back
to line. This can be used indoors – over five metres.

(b) **Last across the line.** Children stand facing along a marked
line. Two further lines (A and B on Figure 3) are approximately 10 metres to left and right. If children stand along one

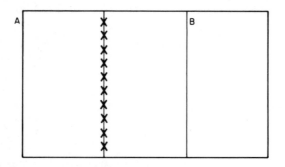

Figure 3   *Last (or First) across the line (example for a netball court)*

*Children (shown by XXX) stand along the line and race to
line A or B according to the signal.*

of the lines of the netball court, facing a touch line, the end of
the court is 10 metres away to one side as is the other one-third
division. The teacher calls '*On your marks*' followed by '*Go*'
or a clap. If 'Go' is called, children run to their left, if the
teacher gives a clap, to their right. 15–20 children at a time can
easily do this. If the netball court has a dotted or coloured line
down the middle, lengthways, the whole class can be accom-
modated, running to the side lines (this extra marking on the
netball court is also useful for other sports activities as it makes
a grid of six areas 10 metres x 7.5 metres).

This list is not exhaustive, and most teachers will be able to think of other running activities to add to it. The point is that *any* running activity is good training for young children. They thrive on enjoyable, varied activity.

## (ii) Sprint relays

These can be an enjoyable form of running activity, even without any technical instruction. Although baton changes may be poorly executed, the children will still run flat out for their stint. After some disastrous change-overs the children may well be able to offer their own suggestions on how to improve the transfer of batons and will then be more receptive of advice.

### Methods of change-over

Several methods of achieving the same objective are possible, all with merit and many enthusiastic supporters. Whichever method is used, it can be successful but, as will be explained later, the actual method used is not the most important factor in a relay change-over.

(1) *Alternate up-sweep*
This is used by many international teams, including Great Britain, and by the majority of club teams in Great Britain.

Number 1 runner runs with baton in the right-hand and places it, with an upward sweep, into the outstretched left hand of 2, who places it into the right hand of 3, who places it into the left hand of 4.

(2) *Alternate down-sweep*
This also has advocates among international squads. The baton is held in, and passed to, the same hand as in the upsweep but, as might be reasonably inferred, it is passed down into the upturned palm.

Both these methods have advantages and disadvantages, but both demand a settled team or squad with the ability to run with a baton in either hand and to run in any order if a team change is needed.

The younger the athlete the more momentous a change in the running order may seem. Some will insist, 'I can't run second, I can only run third.' It only adds to the children's panic

(a)

(b)

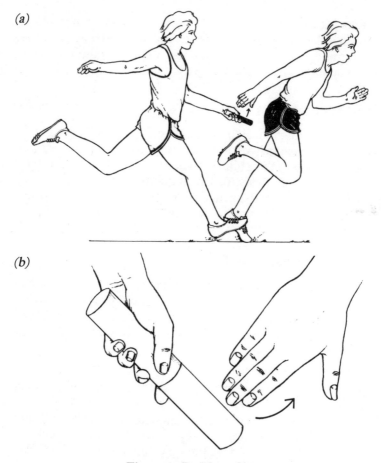

Figure 4   *Position of baton*

if they have to receive a baton in a different hand as well. Ideally a sprinter should be capable of running in any position, of giving and receiving the baton with either hand, and using any method, but this takes time and few schools have ample time. If a teacher is not just preparing at least four teams for inter-school matches, but also class/house teams for Sports Day as well, then the chances of team changes are very high indeed. One must also consider the time factor. Can one justify drilling relay squads to the exclusion of other children and other events? It is suggested that the safest and easiest method be used where children may not be expected to practise to perfection. A sound working model that fulfils this is:

(3) *Right to left up-sweep*
Number 1 runs with the baton in the right hand and passes up into the outstretched left hand of 2 who then changes it to the right hand and passes into the left hand of 3 and so on. Thus, every runner does exactly the same – receives with the left, changes into the right hand and passes with the right hand. As children progress through their schooling, and settled, more experienced team squads develop, then the time may be ripe to change to alternate up-sweep or down-sweep methods, the former being the one encouraged by the British Amateur Athletic Board (B.A.A.B.).

*Problems*
(1) The alternate upsweep method leaves very little free baton to pass to number 4, which involves adjusting the baton while running, preferably by moving the fingers, *not* by knocking the baton against the hip. Experienced athletes, with a larger hand, can do this – but can young children?
(2) The alternate down-sweep involves a rather awkward position of the outstretched arm to receive in the palm. Young children find this hard to hold steady. A further problem occurs when the incoming runner gets too close to the outgoing runner, and a down-sweep pass is not possible. This will happen frequently, so the runners have to improvise, which is risky.
(3) The right to left up-sweep involves changing the baton from one hand to the other, which is not so much risky as involving some inevitable slowing down due to lack of arm drive.

All three methods, therefore, have problems. None is fail-safe, but the right to left up-sweep has the great merit of simplicity and that can save blood, sweat and tears – from both children and teachers.

Whichever method is used, the most important target is to effect the change at speed. To do this:
(1) The outgoing runner must set off fast when the incoming runner shouts 'go' or reaches a check mark (see later for practices).
(2) He/she must put the correct hand back and hold it firmly with a wide 'V' between thumb and forefinger (for up-sweep).
(3) The incoming runner must place the baton firmly and keep sprinting until this is done.

If this is done, whatever method is used, it will be successful. If any of these points go wrong, the method will not work a miracle. Therefore, the phases leading up to the change are vital. The method of transfer is not – it can at best gain about half a metre, but the lead-in work can gain metres.

2　Relay races with baton exchange 1

    (a)  Problems – the outgoing runners in the middle and outside lanes are guilty of looking round for the baton.

    (b)  How much ground has been gained by the inside team can easily be seen.

*Key factors*

**Outgoing runner**

(1) Set off fast at the check mark or on 'Go'.
(2) Put the receiving hand back steadily.
(3) Keep a wide 'V' (or flat palm if down-sweep used).
(4) DON'T look round.

3 Relay races with baton exchange 2

    (a) The exchange is taking place at speed and almost full stretch.
    (b) The outgoing runner is sprinting away at speed after a good change-over.

## Incoming runner
(1) If necessary – shout 'Go' at check mark.
(2) Place the baton firmly when reaching the outgoing runner (i.e. do not run 20 metres with baton outstretched).
(3) Keep sprinting until the baton is exchanged.

## Order of running.
This can affect the team performance. Each team is different and there are no hard and fast rules, but consider these points:
(1) First runner needs to be a reliable starter. He/she can be a poor receiver of the baton if sprinting ability demands a place in the team.

1

2

Figure 5  *Relay baton exchange*

(2) Numbers 2 and 3 need to be strong runners, able to give and take a baton. If all baton changes take place half-way in the take-over zone (page 22), in a 4 x 100 metre relay number 1 will run 100 metres (all with the baton). Numbers 2, 3 and 4 will set off at the back of the box, run approximately ten metres before receiving the baton, then run 100 metres with the baton (total 110 metres). Thus it is particularly important that numbers 2 and 3 do not tire as they are about to change the baton.

(3) The fourth runner does not need to be the fastest but must be the most reliable under pressure, as the temptation to set

3

4

off early is greatest on the last runner. He or she must also be a fighter, able to run with determination, whether closing on rivals ahead or holding off rivals catching up. The best runner is often the most experienced (will have run more races) but, unless he or she fulfils the other needs, should not run last. It is often difficult to convince children of this, as they see their best runner as capable of catching up, forgetting that other schools also have their best runners, who may be even faster.

(4) Two friends will often produce a good change and will cooperate on resolving problems. Two children who do not get on will not achieve the same degree of cooperation.

(5) Avoid extremes of height and speed if possible. Tall to short and fast to slow is preferable to the other way round.

## Baton relay practices

Several batons need to be available. Broom handles, broken shinty sticks or cricket stumps can easily be cut to the right size (30 centimetres). Old rulers can also be taped together.

*Early practice (no baton)*

Group children in pairs. Number 1 stands approximately 4 metres in front of a line such as the starting line on a straight track with a partner 15–20 metres away. On 'Go', 2 sprints in and when the line is crossed number 1 sets off and tries to reach a further line 15 metres away before being touched by 2. Stress that (a) 1 waits until 2 crosses the line, and (b) 1 must run in a straight line – if this is not explained there will always be one who decides to dodge rather than sprint.

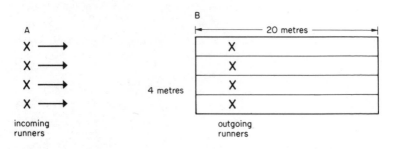

Figure 6   *Relay practices*

       *No baton – A's try to catch B's by the end of 20 metres.*
       *B's start running as A's enter the 20 metre zone.*

With no baton to receive the children have no inhibitions about running off fast. Repeat, having made any adjustments necessary. If number 1 is caught easily, move him/her up a metre or two; if he/she is not caught, move back a metre (or make him/her wait until 2 really does reach the starting line).

Once each child has experienced this chasing and escaping, a further refinement could be that 1 puts the left hand back 5 metres from the finishing line for 2 to touch.

*With a baton*
**Stage 1 – Static** Group in threes, standing 2 paces apart, one behind the other, number 1 with the baton in the right hand. Number 2 puts the left hand back, thumb towards body, wide 'V' between thumb and fingers. Number 1 places the baton up into the 'V', 2 transfers the baton to the right hand, 3 puts the left hand back, 2 passes the baton, 3 changes the baton to the right hand. All three about face and 3 passes to 2, then 2 to 1.

This is a necessary drill, perhaps needed at some stage of most of the early practices, but it should not be overdone, as children are not good at static drills. It can usually be done with effect after some vigorous activity when they appreciate a brief rest.

Encourage children to observe the hand position of their partners – can they place the baton easily? Or is the receiving hand crabbed or twisted?

**Stage 2 – Walking** As for Stage 1 but at a slow walk. Now the passer of the baton calls 'hand' when ready to transfer. Aim to reach this stage fairly quickly.

**Stage 3 – Jogging** As 1 and 2.

**Stage 4 – Jogging in fours** This can be done round the track or playground on the same lines as Chain Run (see Sprinting, page 27). Number 1 calls 'hand', transfers the baton and then sprints to the front. Number 2, when he/she sees 1 is at the front and jogging, calls 'hand' and transfers to 3, then sprints to the front and so on. Thus there is no need to turn around.

**Stage 5 – Sprinting and check marks** If the first practice, without batons, has been covered, this stage is fairly easy. The children have got the idea of check marks and sprinting off hard, and putting the left hand back. Stages 1–4 have accustomed them to the transfer of a baton. To marry the two, repeat the final part of the first practice (without batons), but with a baton exchanged rather than touching hands. It may help if the outgoing runner keeps his/her hand back all the time (not very good for sprinting – but children are less likely to put the wrong hand back and, if they do, the incoming runner can shout), or if the incoming runner can call 'hand' as he/she nears the outgoing runner.

The first check mark is at 4 metres, as before, then adjustments can be made. The aim should be to receive the baton, at speed, early in the second half of the 20 metre zone. This is safe – a change near the end is, of course, correct but allows little room for error.

*Baton relay races*
These can take place throughout the preceding baton practices, as they will add interest and generate enthusiasm. A race to begin and end each practice can indicate growing skill. As mentioned earlier, the lack of skill will not mar the effort.
1 **Pairs relay (2 x 40 metres)** Number 1 sprints 40 metres, passes to 2 who completes the course. Three races of five pairs can cover the whole class. They can then race back, 2 passing to 1.
2 **Shuttle relay with baton**
(a) On a netball court, using the centre third as a take-over zone, number 1 sprints from the centre section to the end, turns and sprints back, passing over to 2 within the centre section. Number 2 sprints to the other end, turns and sprints back and passes to 3 who continues and passes to 4. Use the

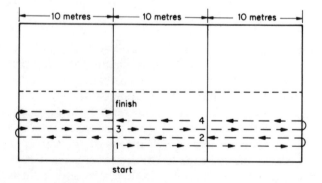

*Figure 7  Shuttle relay with baton change, using a netball court*

> *Use the centre zone (10 metres) as the take-over zone.*
> *Each runner runs 30 metres (20 metres + 10 metres) plus up to 10 metres within the zone.*

start line as the finish line as well (see Figure 7). This can also be done over about 40 metres on the track if lines are drawn every 10 metres.

(b) As for a normal shuttle relay, except each team has a skittle/cone/non-participant 10 metres behind the scratch line. Each runner runs past his scratch line, round the marker and passes to the next runner. A course of 20 metres is adequate.

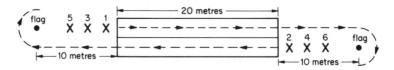

Figure 8 *Shuttle relay with baton change*

*Each runner goes round the flag and passes the baton to the next runner.*

3 **Combined shuttle/baton relay** (see Figure 9) Make up teams of four. Each child runs 40 metres. Number 1 sprints 40 metres and passes to 2 who continues for 40 metres. Change between 2 and 3 is a shuttle change (touch). Number 3 already has a baton and sprints back to 4 who goes on to finish. In the second race, 4 becomes 1, 1 is 2 and so on. Thus each runner eventually runs in each position and in four races. The runners will each have started once, passed a baton twice and received a baton twice.

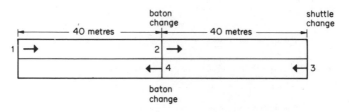

Figure 9 *Combined shuttle and baton relay*

4 **'Normal' relay** So far a circular track has not been mentioned. It can be a handicap in the early stages of practice, as inexperienced, confused children are spread round the track, so it is advisable to cover most of the early practices on the straight where all are within earshot.

Most junior schools, if possible, have a 300-metre track and

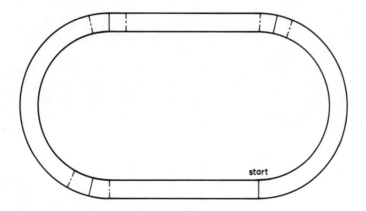

Figure 10   *4 × 100 metre relay take-over zones (no acceleration zone)*

run 4 x 75 metre relays. Variations exist. Some District Sports are held on cinder tracks and so 4 x 100 metre relays can be run. If this is so, athletes *must* experience sprinting 110 metres.

The take-over zone, within which batons must be exchanged, is 20 metres on a 400-metre track and is usually the same on a 300-metre track, but is sometimes reduced to 15 metres. In addition, an acceleration zone of 10 metres is marked on a cinder track, but does not have much relevance for under-12s, and although it is marked on Figure 11 for information, it is suggested that it should be ignored.

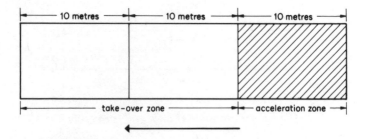

Figure 11   *Take-over and acceleration zones*

If the track has a mark every 75 metres but no box/zone, stand the runners on this mark, otherwise stand them at the back of the zone.

A problem ocurs when marking check marks. With spikes,

a mark can be scratched on grass, but not with plimsolls. One solution is to stand the runners 4 to 5 metres (as needed) inside the zone, thus making the back of the zone the check mark.

When sending children to their take-over positions, it is worth, at first, putting them in their correct lanes and getting them to walk round, in the lanes, to their marks. This is time-consuming, but not as time-consuming as having to run over and sort out confusion at each take-over area. It may also help if, when the track is marked, the numerals 1, 2, 3 and 4 can be marked in each lane at each take-over point.

Children who stay in lanes after they have passed a baton on a straight track will, nevertheless, cut across when running on a circular one. For safety, as well as to avoid disqualification, insist that they should '*stay in lanes*' until everyone has gone past.

## (iii) Middle distance (600 metres to 3000 metres), cross-country and fun runs

There is no problem in young children running fairly long distances *provided* they can slow down or even stop when they want to. Problems occur when they are forced to *race* at a speed beyond their ability, or continue when tired. Before any child attempts timed runs or races he or she *must* have a good background of steady running and running activities.

### Skills

The most important skill for any middle distance runner, of any age, is that of pace judgment – that is, the ability to run at the fastest economic pace that can be maintained throughout the distance. This can only come through experience by trial and error. Running action is not too important, for an exaggerated stride or arm action soon leads to fatigue and this makes a runner modify the style, often without instruction, although many will benefit from advice.

### Conditioning

1 *Steady running*
The best way to develop this is regularly to start P.E./games lessons with a steady run. At first this may be just once round

the football pitch, or three times round the netball court. A child of eight or over who genuinely cannot jog steadily for about 250 to 300 metres is in need of either medical advice or a gradual but definite increase in physical activity. Such children certainly should not participate in any vigorous activity until they have been medically checked.

This opening run, after a few lessons, can be gradually increased. Later the keener ones may respond to the challenge of, say, running three laps of the pitch whilst the rest run two.

This preliminary jog is also a valuable warm-up for any sporting activity.

## 2  Pursuit races

Children are paired off by ability (often if they choose their own partners they tend to choose a partner of similar general sports ability) and spread round the track, half football pitch, or netball court, and stand opposite each other. On 'Go' they run anti-clockwise and try to catch up on their partner. Call a halt after three to five minutes, the winner in each pair being the one who has closed up. Usually, if one child cannot keep running, he or she stops and walks and allows himself/herself to be caught, although often the partner will stop and walk too. When one starts again, so does the other.

It is advisable to place flags, cones, or non-participating children at corners.

## 3  Overtaking

Spread the class round the track/pitch/court and run for three to five minutes. Children score one point for each child they overtake. Some will exaggerate, of course, but employ non-participants to check on any you suspect of exaggerating claims.

## 4  Against the clock

Spread the class round the course and run for three to five minutes. Each child counts how many laps are completed and, at the end, how many quarter laps (complete sides of court/pitch). Thus, when the activity is repeated, children have individual targets to aim for and can measure improvement.

For activities 2, 3 and 4, the duration of the runs can gradually be increased. If a track is used, two groups could run at a time, those using the inside lane running for five minutes, those in lanes 3 or 4 for 10 minutes. A football pitch, or even the netball court, can be divided into two courses.

## 5 *Chain run (or trains)*
In groups of four, children jog round track/pitch in single file. When the whistle is blown, the last child sprints to the front and slows to a jog. When all are jogging, the whistle is blown again and the activity repeated. With experience, children can do this in groups of up to ten and, in time, can judge when the back marker reaches the front without need of a whistle.

## 6 *Relays*
(1) **Shuttle relays.** As for sprinting but run through three to four times without pause – as the last runner finishes, number 1 restarts. Teams of five, seven, or nine help this to go smoothly.

(2) **Continuous relays.** Teams of seven to ten are spread round the track/pitch with the last runner alongside number 1. Number 1 runs to 2, who runs to 3 and so on. The 'spare' runner restarts lap two and runs to 1 who is standing where he/she handed over. Run for three to four laps or a fixed time (five minutes, building up to ten minutes).

Warn runners not to race flat out or they will not manage several repetitions.

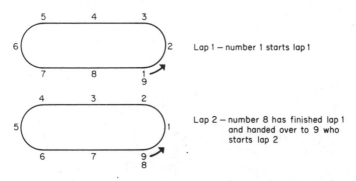

Figure 12  *Continuous relay (example for 9 runners)*

(3) **Distance relays.** Few junior schools have large fields and even fewer have suitable cross-country courses nearby where children can be adequately supervised. Thus they are reduced to running round and round the school field which soon becomes boring. This can be enlivened by making the race a longer distance relay, each runner completing a stint of 500 to 800 metres. To increase variety, low obstacles to be jumped can be introduced, such as old car tyres, corner flags across

cones or skittles, old benches or mats, and similar objects. If the course can involve running through the long jump pit, so much the better. It also adds to the interest if runners can go behind buildings, out of sight, and then re-emerge. Unobstructed pathways within the school grounds may also be used.

Teams of three or four are probably the best size or too large a gap between teams develops.

### 7  *Five Star Cross-Country Award Scheme*

Particular reference should be made to this scheme (explained in Section III, Incentive Schemes, pages 76–7) as it embraces training as well as time trials and races.

## (iv)  Hurdles

This is not an event frequently held for under-12s, but it is one that children will enjoy and can be attempted without several flights of expensive hurdles. Cones or skittles with canes across are quite adequate and sometimes secondary schools have hurdles that can no longer be raised above 61 centimetres (2 feet). This is high enough for under 12s – too high for many.

### Skills

Hurdling is a rhythm event. The objective should be smooth running, over and between hurdles. If the build-up stages are followed, the better athletes will develop this rhythm and should be encouraged to drive their leading leg over the hurdles. At this level no further instruction is needed. The naturals will fall into a reasonable style. Those who do not achieve fluency will, nevertheless, enjoy another form of running activity.

*Progression*

1 **Ground level obstacles** (canes, shinty sticks, small mats) 4 to 5 metres apart.

Children run over three to four flights. Aim to build up a rhythm of striding not jumping. If two or three lines of obstacles are used, gradually adjust spacings – for example, lane A: 4 metres apart, lane B: 4.5 metres apart, lane C: 5 metres apart. As the group gains confidence, each lane can have the obstacles moved a further half metre apart.

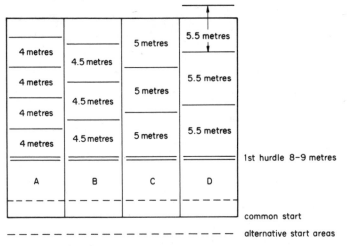

Figure 13 *Hurdles grid for beginners*

*Short striders in lane A – if they cope, try B.*
*Medium striders in lane B – if they cope, try C.*
*Long striders in lane C.*
*When those in lane C cope easily, move them to lane D.*
*Adjust spacings as needed (5.5 metres is not the maximum).*
*Adjust the starting point for each child as needed.*

2 **Low height obstacles** (canes or shinty sticks placed on bean bags, margarine cartons, old books, then on yoghurt cartons, empty tins, and so on).

Encourage children to find some rhythm in running, trying to lead with the same leg each time (i.e. three strides between each obstacle), although those who can lead easily with either may develop into a 400-metre hurdler in six to eight years' time.

Adjust spacings as for 1.

3 **Medium height** 30–40cm (canes across cones or skittles, held in position if needed by a bean bag, or across cones with a groove).

Develop as before. Better athletes will need up to 6 metres spacing between hurdles. This is as far as most under 12s will reach but, if hurdles are available, progress to

4 **Hurdles at 61 centimetres (2 feet)** This will depend on space, hurdles and time. Usually only a small group will be involved. As in previous stages children should be able to

LEAN

Figure 14  *Hurdles clearance*

adjust the spacing between hurdles to suit their stride. Encourage fluent hurdling, not jumping. As well as driving the leading leg over the hurdle, better athletes may also be capable of pulling the knee of the trailing leg round, rather than picking the knee up, but this is not worth worrying too much about at this stage. It is better to leave this alone than to try to achieve the 'hurdle' position, with the trailing thigh at 90° to the lead leg. This can result in children freezing in this position and floating over the hurdle. The trailing leg is never still.

5  **Competition hurdles** For 12- to 13-year-olds who are likely to compete in hurdles races. The hurdles are gradually moved to the height and spacing of the competition (see Section IV, Competition, pages 97–8). Emphasis is on the trailing leg mentioned in 4 above.

A useful drill to get the feel of this is for the children to walk down the left side of the hurdles (assuming the left leg is the leading leg) and as they step past the hurdle to bring the trailing leg over, thigh at 90° to the leading leg and parallel to the ground. Once they can walk over the hurdle fluently in this manner, progress to jogging.

A second drill is to jog down the centre of the hurdles lane and at each hurdle drive the lead leg over and pull trailing leg round.

In both drills the pace is such that the skill can be concentrated on and refined. It is also easy for the teacher to watch and spot errors, and of course good points. Most practices will be over three to four flights for convenience but some *must* be at racing distance.

# B WALKING

Of all athletic events, walking is the hardest to judge correctly. Walking is defined as having unbroken contact with the ground: before the rear foot leaves the ground the front foot must make contact with it. The leg must also be straightened in each stride (no bent leg scuttling).

At under 13 level, it is probably easiest to insist on the heel of the front foot striking the ground first. It is difficult to run on the heels.

A walking race can provide variety and enjoyment. Both the Ten-Step and Five-Star schemes include walking and it is recommended they are used as time trials not races, on the same lines as middle-distance.

# C JUMPING

## Safety

1 *Sand pits* must be dug regularly, raked and free from debris – and rakes.

2 If a *landing area* is used (as for high jump) it must be large enough to ensure children do not jump over it. An area 5 × 2.5 metres is recommended. If a slightly smaller area is used, the surrounds should be protected by gymnastic mats.

3 The *Fosbury Flop* (a backward bending style of jump) must

*not* be attempted unless a foam landing area is in use. Many
Local Education Authorities (L.E.A.s) prohibit this type of
jump in junior schools and it should not be taught except by a
P.E. specialist or qualified coach.

4 *High jump bars* can be painful to land on; ones of circular
section are less painful than the triangular ones, and are
recommended.

5 *Take-off boards* should be flush with the run up.

6 *Discipline* of the jumpers is essential. There must be no
fooling about, no attempts to put off the jumper, no jumping
before the previous jumper has got clear.


## (i)  Long jump

The appeal of running and jumping into sand makes this a
popular event, even with children of little ability.


## Skills

Far and away the most important skills are a controlled run up
and vigorous take-off from the board. If these are achieved,
style in the air will make only a slight difference to the distance
jumped, and concentration on what to do in the air will usually
adversely affect a young athlete's run up and take-off. Certainly the Hitch Kick has no place at all for under 13s – or for
that matter with any athlete jumping much less than 6 metres.

*Take-off*
The foundation is laid in a normal indoor P.E. lesson. The
children should perform a range of jumping and landing
activities. Among these would be running a few steps and
jumping high in the air. Encourage use of both left and right
foot to establish preference. Stress:

1 Rock from heel to toe for take-off.
2 Sink the hips and slightly bend the knee.
3 Swing up with the arms – hold head and chest high (not
  back).
4 Drive the free knee up.
5 Emphasise the need for 'squashy' landings by giving at the
knees.

A standing long jump at this stage also encourages vigorous
take-off and use of arms.

**Run up**
**Stage I:** Having chosen which is the take-off leg, children run three to four strides to the side of the pit and jump high in the air. If the side of the pit is used, three or four lines of children can practise – thus there is no waiting. Emphasise: (a) for safety, walk out of the pit at the far side – do not turn toward the ends into the path of another jumper; and (b) do not run up until the child ahead is clear.

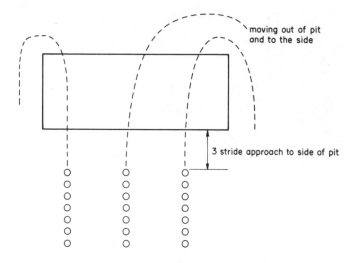

Figure 15  *Long jump – group practice for three stride approach*

*Practice for a large group, using the side of the pit*

**Stage 2:** Extend run up to five strides and aim to take off near the edge.
**Stage 3:** Change to traditional use of pit and board (reduce numbers – see lesson plan, page 59). From a five stride approach, aim to take off *near* the board without shuffling.
**Stress:** Start the run up with the take-off leg so that that leg reaches the board area. Adjust the starting position to gain accuracy.
**Stage 4:** Increase the run up to seven, then nine strides. A nine stride approach is as much as most juniors will handle with accuracy, although some may well be capable of 11 to 13.

At all stages continually stress smooth, even run up, and points 1 to 4 from the indoor practice for take-off (page 32).

4  Long jump, with good height on take-off, by a nine-year-old. Note the
child recording.

*Practices*
1  To gain height, a spring-board can be placed on the take-off
board. A five stride approach and vigorous take-off gives time
in the air to extend the body. Although this is, to some extent,
an unrealistic practice, it gives children the feel of the skill
they are attempting. Children who are capable gymnasts may
at first try to take off using both feet, but will soon adapt (and
then try a single foot take-off in gymnastics!).
2  An object (say a P.E. band) held from a pole above the pit
can also be used to encourage extension – the athlete stretches
up to reach the band. This is preferable to an object placed
above the ground that has to be jumped over – children will
tend to look down and only concern themselves with getting
over it.
3  With capable jumpers, the next stage (to improve distance)
is to shoot the feet forward on landing, but few master the
more important basics sufficiently to move on to this. Those
that do can be encouraged by placing an object (say a leaf) in
the sand at their normal distance. They then try to push their
heels beyond this object.

# (ii) Triple jump (Hop, step and jump)

This event is an interesting, but physically demanding, development from the long jump; it is not recommended for under 12s and should be covered sparingly with all young athletics. Footwear with good, shock-absorbing soles is essential. The Women's A.A.A. does not permit girls to compete in the Triple Jump.

## Skills

A background of long jumping is assumed and the progressions for a controlled run up and take-off should have been covered. The Triple Jump is three even phases of effort and a good performance can be heard clearly –

*Bang* (hop) ★ ★ ★ *Bang* (step) ★ ★ ★ *Bang* (jump)

If too much effort is put into the hop,

*Bang* (hop) ★ ★ ★ ★ *Bang* (step) ★ *Bang* (jump)

the step phase is only a very short one to recover balance and overall distance is lost.

The hop phase is controlled and the vigorous vertical lift of the long jump is replaced by a lower trajectory to maintain momentum.

The step is aided by the front leg knee being brought through high, and this enables a controlled jump at the end which would not be possible if the front foot were stretched too far in front.

Aim to keep the body upright and the feet flat on landing, with knees slightly bent.

*Progressions*

1 **Standing triple jump** on grass or mats, thus establishing (a) the coordination of the three phases, and (b) the favourite take-off leg. If a child cannot hop to start (and many children cannot; they will take a step first), suggest that he or she holds the free leg at the start so that a hop is the only means of progress.

2 **Three stride run up** to take off into the pit from the side (as in long jump) using three or four groups.

3 **Five to seven stride run up** from the side of the pit.

4 **Eleven stride run up** to board.

As the distances achieved will vary far more than the long jump, one child may take off 5 metres from the pit and find his step lands in the pit whereas another cannot reach the pit from 5 metres after the jump. To solve this problem the children need to be in ability groups after Stage 1, the Standing Triple Jump.

Thus the top group might have a take-off some 6 metres from the side of the pit, and the less able athletes a take-off progressively nearer. These distances need to be varied according to the stage of progression and ability of the class. In competitions two or more take-off boards may be used and competitors can nominate which one they wish to take off from.

Each stage of progression should end with simple competitions, either individual or team.

# (iii) High jump

This is an event that requires perhaps the greatest organisation and supervision. After the early practices, it is best taught in small groups of six to eight.

## Skills

If asked to jump an obstacle, most children will jump it from the frontal approach. A few will approach from the side and scissor kick over. Of the two, the second, the *Scissors*, is the more efficient.

The athlete approaches from the side (25° to 30°) and kicks the near leg vigorously up and over the centre of the bar (opens the scissors). This is followed by bringing the far foot up and over (close the scissors). The reaction to this move is to bring the near foot down into the landing area. This is simple to perform and is the basic technique for jumpers.

The *Fosbury Flop* is a backward bending jump over the bar, and for safety reasons most L.E.A.s prohibit its use in junior schools. If a proficient scissors jumper eventually concentrates on High Jump, then the conversion to the Fosbury (with suitable landing area and coaching by a qualified coach or P.E. specialist) is not difficult.

Two other techniques involving a layout along the bar are the *Straddle* and the rather older *Western Roll*. Both are more efficient than the Scissors, but the time taken to teach these skills so they can be performed at a height comparable to the child's best scissors jump cannot be justified for under-13s and should not be taught at any age except by a qualified coach or P.E. specialist. The children are usually so concerned about the skill in the air that they forget about getting *high* first.

When performing a simple scissors the emphasis is on a *high* kick; the rest follows. No potential high jumper is going to be retarded by a background of scissor jumping, but a poorly taught Straddle or Western Roll could take a long time to correct.

*Practices*
As for the long jump, early phases are taught indoors during a P.E. lesson.

1 **Free practice** – three to four light steps and kick high into the air (imagine kicking at a ball at chest height) and land softly. This establishes the take-off leg. Revise long jump skills of rocking heel-toe on take-off, use of arms, sinking of hips before take-off.

2 **Free practice of scissor jumping** over *low* obstacles (benches, canes on top of cones, skipping rope held lightly by partners) and landing softly.

3 **Ropes** held slightly higher (40 to 50 centimetres) and landing on good mats.

4 **Outdoors** (or small group indoors on crash mats). Equipment – high jump stands and bar or rope, landing mats or sand pit.

(a) Low height – three to five stride approach.

(b) Increase the height to the ability of the worst jumper (that means no failures).

Number the jumpers and insist on strict order of jumping. Allow adjustments of the angle of run up. If it is too shallow, the jumper travels along the bar. If it is too steep, the scissors is not effective.

The problem now occurs that bedevils high jump teaching and coaching. If there is a wide range of ability in the long jump (2.5 metres to 4 metres) the 4 metre jumper is not in any way restricted from performing a 4 metre jump by the 2.5 metres jump preceding and vice-versa. However in the high jump a bar at one metre plus is daunting to the child struggling at 70 centimetres, and 70 centimetres is little incentive to the one metre plus jumper.

After early practices, it is usually best to group high jumpers by ability. The problem will still occur, but not to such an extent. Every practice does *not* have to be a competition. When a height is reached that most can clear, count who can clear it the most times.

A rope has been suggested as an alternative to a bar – this is not a throw-back to pre-war days but a realistic aid to greater success in high jump teaching. The advantages of a rope are:

1 There are no inhibitions – it will not hurt.

2 It is easier to replace on stands than a bent, twisted bar.

3 It is harder to dislodge – therefore more achieve success in a *teaching* situation.

4 Minor adjustments to the height – plus or minus 10 centimetres – can be made by adjusting the tension of the rope. Thus the less able athletes can continue jumping.

5 A metre stick can quickly measure the low point of the rope – contrast with measuring a twisted and bent bar.

6 The bar is saved for competition or those preparing for competition.

NOTE: An elastic 'rope' is now on the market with alternate black and white stripes which is even better than a conventional rope for practice.

Once children can clear one metre, they can transfer to using a bar. Those unable to do so are not likely to suffer because their jumps are not absolutely accurate. The first five points listed above all result in more jumps per child in any given time – a very great benefit.

## (iv) Standing jumps and general jumping activities

Many hopping and bounding activities can be used to provide excellent conditioning for high jump, long jump and triple jump, and give variety. They can also be used by children in small groups without continual supervision, thus freeing the teacher to concentrate on a long jump, high jump or triple jump group. Obviously the groups should change places after a time.

1 *Standing long jump* (Ten-Step and Five-Star)
Begin with feet together and toes behind a line (long jump board, or a line on the field, playground, or gym, or a rope).

Measure from behind the rearmost point of landing to front

of line. A mat for landing prevents jarring – if you are working outdoors, a discarded gym mat can enjoy a new lease of life.

*Team competitions* are made by combining total distance from each team or pair. An interesting variation is: number 1 jumps, then 2 puts his/her toes to the landing point and takes a jump, 3 and the rest follow in the same way. Thus the winning team can be established without measuring, just marking.

2 *Standing three spring jumps* (both feet together – 'Kangaroo Jumps')

This activity involves three successive long jumps without a pause. Team competitions can be run as above.

3 *Standing triple jump* (hop, step and jump – 'same, other, both')

Coordination often causes problems. It sometimes helps if half-effort jumps are performed to gain the rhythm. Team competitions as above.

4 *15 metre hop*

Hop 15 metres *on the same leg* against the clock, or make into a race or shuttle relay.

5 *10 metre power hop*

How few hops to cover 10 metres?

6 *10 metre spring jumps*

How few spring jumps?

Both these activities are very strenuous – only two to three attempts should be made at any time. Team competitions can be made from them by totalling jumps.

7 *Standing high jumps*

Jump over *low* obstacles. Jumps can be scissors or two feet. A landing mat is very desirable.

8 *Hopping/jumping into hoops*

Two, three or four hoops are placed touching one another, and children hop or jump from one to the other. How many in 'x' seconds?

9 *Combination jumps*

Free practice, putting together the hop, step, jump types of jump (say hop, hop, step, step, jump, jump – or hop, step, hop, step, jump). Children can work in groups of three or four and compare distances by simple markers or measuring.

# D THROWS

As will have been clear from the introduction, the aim of this book is to assist non-specialist P.E. teachers, and it is not likely that they will have much need to teach shot, discus, or javelin. However, in schools catering for 12- and 13-year-olds a non-specialist may be assisting with athletics and a situation could arise when he/she may be expected to impart some instruction in these three throws. Therefore the basic beginnings of these events, involving standing throws, are briefly covered. The main emphasis in this section is on the cricket or rounders ball throwing which is needed for the eight to 11 age groups. The general throwing and strength activities are suitable for all throws.

## Safety

1 At all times regard throwing implements for what they are – dangerous weapons. They are not toys and must not be used for play.
2 At all times supervise young children with javelins and discus. With shot and cricket/rounders ball, selected groups, after careful instruction, may be allowed short periods of unsupervised practice – but never out of sight.
3 All throwers must stand back from the throwing line/circle and not step forward until instructed.
4 No throw should take place until instructed and only when appointed judges are in front of the throwing area and are watching. Emphasise the dual responsibility of this – not just of the teacher but of the thrower as well. In competition, a warning signal (say a hooter) should be sounded.
5 No implements are to be retrieved until instructed. In class teaching this will be when all have thrown.
6 Never run while carrying implements.

### Javelin
1 Extra care is needed in carrying a javelin as it is sharp at both ends. It must be carried vertically, not at the trail.
2 Extra care is needed when a javelin is left anywhere. If left stuck in the ground it may tilt, and thus the tail could be at eye level.

## Discus

Due to the rotational nature of the throw (even standing throws) the area of potential danger is greater due to early or late release. The early release is the more common, so the danger area is greater to the right of a right-hander. It is advisable to segregate left- and right-handed throwers.

Children must be instructed in safety procedures and constantly reminded of them. Children disobeying instructions, even accidentally, must be disciplined. This could range from exclusion from the rest of the session to a complete ban from athletics, depending on the nature of the offence.

*Essential reading* is 'Safety Measures in Athletics', a pamphlet produced by the A.A.A. Schools' Consultative Council available from the A.A.A., Francis House, Francis Street, London, SW1P 1LD, or L.E.As.

# (i) Throwing the cricket/rounders ball

The foundation for throwing is again laid indoors. Using lightweight air-flow or play balls or foam bags, a great deal of throwing can be done without the problem of retrieving balls or causing damage. Most stages of practice for safety do not involve cricket/rounder balls.

**Skills** (for right-handed throwers)
**Stage 1:**
(1) Hold a team band in the right hand.
(2) Stand sideways to the direction of throw, feet shoulder width apart, left foot turned to the front.
(3) Point the left arm in direction of throw, look along arm.
(4) Raise the right hand to the ear, elbow up.
(5) Bend the right knee slightly.
(6) Lash with the team band, bringing hips then shoulders round, by straightening the right leg and pulling the left arm back. The lashing action is particularly valuable for girls who tend to push rather than throw. ←
**Stage 2:** Repeat as above but use a play ball. Work with a partner, throwing to one another. For accuracy, 'throw the fingers at the target'. As the throwing gets more vigorous the right arm is taken further back, but check a tendency to throw with a straight arm (this is bowling).

Introduce throwing at targets – skittles, hoops, circles on a wall and so on.

**Stage 3:** Step and throw.

(1) Face the direction of the throw.

(2) Step forward with the left foot into the throwing position (stage 1 but in one movement).

(3) Throw.

(4) Then introduce three steps (left, right, left) and throw.

**Stage 4:** Run up and throw.

(1) Three steps as above – but a little faster.

(2) Five steps. Many will not reach this stage while still being able to coordinate; if this is the case, be content with a three step run up. Introduce left, right, left, and *slight* jump on to right, left – throw. Encourage the final step to be a little longer.

(3) For capable throwers, increase the run up to seven or even nine steps. This is sufficient for a controlled throw.

At all times insist on a smooth, continuous run up and throw, not run up, stop and throw.


# (ii) Putting the shot – simple progressions (for a right-handed thrower)

In the early stages, use the lightest shot available (about 2 kilogrammes), or tennis balls filled with cement. This enables the child to have control, confidence and success.

**Stage 1:**

(1) Hold and push. The stance is facing the direction of the throw with feet shoulder width apart. The shot is held in the base of the fingers, not in the palm, and placed into the child's neck just below the right ear. The right elbow and upper arm is held parallel to the ground. The left arm is held up. The basic shot putting movement from this position is a vigorous *push* from the neck.

(2) Having mastered the push, encourage children to twist the right shoulder backwards and then twist vigorously forward and push the shot away.

**Stage 2:**

(1) The stance is sideways to the direction of the throw, feet apart as before.

Figure 16  *Standing shot put*

(2) The toe of the left shoe is approximately level with the right heel.

(3) Bend the right knee and take a position of balance with the chin, right knee and right toe in a vertical line. Eyes should be looking back.

(4) Thrust from the right foot, rotate the hips and shoulders and thrust the shot away as in stage 1.

(5) Emphasise the sequence of movement – leg, hips, shoulders, arm.

(6) Emphasise the high point of release, aided by keeping the left arm up.

(7) If the thrust is vigorous, the right leg will follow through to the throwing line or stop board.

This is the basic standing putting position, and most children will achieve distances with this method which they cannot match when trying a shift or glide across the circle unless they are very quick, coordinated learners or spend quite some time practising. A shift or glide still brings the child into the standing put position, therefore this is a basic technique worth spending some time perfecting.

**Large group situations** A shot put circle is a 2.135 metre (7 foot) diameter circle of concrete. It is unlikely that a school has more than two or three – usually only one. Therefore when the teacher has a large group a throwing line can be used. Up to eight children, 3 metres apart, can throw at a time. A second and third group can wait their turns, 5 metres back from the line. As the group progresses, a makeshift stop board can be made from old goal posts, held in position by long nails or pegs.

## (iii)  Discus – progressions

(1) **Control** To allow children to gain confidence in handling a discus, use rubber quoits. Allow children free (but supervised) practice in rolling a quoit along the ground by spinning it off the index finger and flighting the quoit in the air with a round arm throw.

(2) **Standing throw** For class use, rubber or wooden discoi are better than the wood and metal competition ones. The rubber ones are the correct weight, though the wooden ones are a little light (these can be manufactured in the school woodwork shop).

*Hold* the discus in the right hand with the pads of the finger tips just overlapping the rim and fingers spread. Steady the discus if needed (and most children will need to) with the left hand.

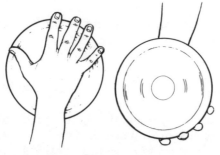

Figure 17   *Grip for the discus*

*Stand* with the left shoulder sideways to the direction of throw with feet shoulder width apart, left toe level with the right heel.

Gently *swing* the discus to the right and behind, keeping the arm up, and then swing back to the front by the left shoulder and steady with the left hand. As the discus moves behind, find the position of balance as for the shot with the chin, right knee and toes in a vertical line.

*The throw* is achieved without preliminary swings – they are just to establish control and the feel of the correct position.

Swing back into the standing throw position and thrust as in the shot from the right leg, rotate the hips and then the shoulders, bringing the discus through behind the line of the shoulders.

Figure 18  *Standing discus throw*

The first few throws should be below full effort to encourage flighting the discus and avoid it spinning over and over.

As with the shot, most children will throw as far, or even further, with a standing throw as with a running turn until considerable practice has been put in. The running turn still brings the thrower into the standing throw position.

**Large group situations** An inexperienced teacher would be best advised not to attempt to teach the discus to a large group. A group of ten is quite large enough. As in the shot, insufficient circles will be available and so a throwing line can be used, but children should throw one at a time and only step up to the line when called. If the children wait behind the thrower but 2 to 3 metres to the left (see Figure 19), the throws can commence from the right hand end of the line and work towards the left. After throwers have had their turn, they should retreat ten metres; thus the danger area (to the right) for the next thrower is clear. Any left-handed throwers should be at the left-hand end of the line.

This way of organising throwing is regimented but *safe*.

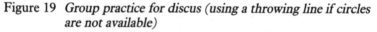

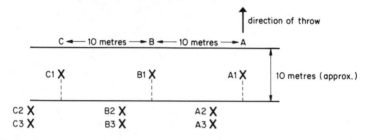

Figure 19    *Group practice for discus (using a throwing line if circles are not available)*

> *A 1 throws then retreats behind the line (A 3).*
> *B 1 throws and retreats.*
> *C 1 then throws and retreats.*
> *A 2, B 2, C 2 then step forward and throw in turn.*
> *Any left-handers should go into group C.*

## (iv)  Javelin – progressions

**The grip** The easiest grip is to hold the javelin as if to spear an enemy. Most children will then be holding the javelin in the correct position for throwing. Slight adjustments should be made to place the index finger behind the cord grip to give extra purchase, and to lie the javelin down the palm, not across.

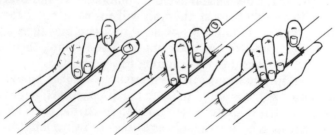

Figure 20    *(a)  Grip for javelin*
       *A and B are usual holds; C is also possible.*

*(b) Javelin throw*

**Standing throw**
(1) Stance is with the left foot forward. Draw the javelin back behind the head, keeping the right palm upwards.
(2) Thrust the javelin forward at the ground 5 to 10 metres away.
(3) Progress to throwing for distance. At this stage, don't worry if the javelin does not land point first.
**Three to five stride run up** Unlike shot and discus, a short run up will improve a javelin throw in the early stages. Progress as for the cricket ball – one step and throw, three steps and throw, three steps with the third step being slightly longer, five steps and throw from a longer fifth stride.

Do not allow the run up to be faster than the child can control, which would result in five steps, stop and throw.

5   An example of what can be achieved by a young athlete in the javelin
event: throwing arm brought back straight, leading foot planted in line
with the throw (not turned to the left as many inexperienced throwers
do), good follow through, and stopping just short of the throwing line.

POINTS TO NOTE

(1) Novice throwers often plant the left foot sideways in the final stride. This can lead to a twisted knee, so emphasise the plant of the feet in a forward direction.

(2) The javelin should be brought back as far as possible, with the throwing arm straight. For those who lack the strength or mobility to do this, insist that the elbow is kept pointing forwards and the palm up. If children get into the habit of bringing their elbow out or throwing 'round the corner' they run a risk of injury.

(3) Ensure children start their run up with sufficient room to stop before the line after throwing.

**Large group situations** As with the discus, inexperienced teachers should avoid taking large groups for practice. A group of ten is quite large enough. Using one long throwing line, children can throw in turn or two or three at a time in the early stages, provided they are 4 to 5 metres apart. Discipline is *essential*.

The early progressions to emphasise the upward facing palm and extended arm can be dealt with using weighted throwing balls (for example, old tennis balls filled with cement), but care must be taken not to use implements that are too heavy. There is on the market a shampoo in a plastic container with finger and thumb grips indented which could have been designed with the javelin thrower in mind. Used containers can be filled to the right weight (up to 400 grammes) with sand and used for throwing practice.

## (v) Throwing activities

(1) **Target throwing** from 10 to 15 metres with tennis balls or bean bags at skittles or cones or cricket stumps, or (if away from a classroom) tin cans which make a rewarding sound when hit.

(2) **Throwing and catching with a partner** (use tennis balls). Which pair can stand furthest apart and still catch?

(3) **Buzz ball.** Teams of six to ten, armed with play balls, face each other across No Man's Land – for example, the centre area of a badminton court. A football is placed between the teams. The aim is to drive the ball over the opponents' line (no touching the ball). With large numbers (say 30), make up four teams of seven to eight. Teams 1 and 2 throw, teams 3 and 4

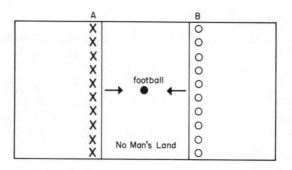

Figure 21   *Buzz ball (throwing games using a badminton court)*

> *Using play balls, drive the football over the opponent's line.*

retrieve balls and return to throwers. (Either allow any type of throw or insist on over-arm.)

(4) **Knee ball** (up to 15 to 16 a side). Using a badminton court, teams face each other across No Man's Land (centre area). Each team has a play ball or a medium-size rubber ball (half way between tennis ball and football). The aim is to strike the members of the other team below the knee. On being struck, players retire to the back of badminton court *behind* the other team. They are not out, and the ball can be thrown to them and they can then throw at opponents. The winning team is the one to clear their opponents out of the starting zone, but until this happens everyone is still involved. As with Buzz Ball, over-arm throwing can be optional or compulsory.

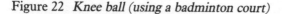

Figure 22   *Knee ball (using a badminton court)*

> *Those behind their opponents have been struck, but are not 'out'; they can receive a pass from a team mate and throw at an opponent.*

6 A seated football throw, with a child taking responsibility for recording.

(5) **Seated soccer throw** (Ten-Step). Sit behind line, ball in *two* hands. Throw from above the head.

(6) **Standing soccer throw** (Ten-Step). Throw from above the head with two hands.

(7) **Standing netball throw**. Push or chest pass style, or one handed shot put style.

(8) **Sling ball**

(1) Throw a football or rugby ball either round arm or one-handed over-arm.

(2) If a 'sling ball' is available (usually only in Scotland), this can be used. A sling ball is a weighted ball with a handle. Various weights can be obtained.

(9) **Two-handed sling** (rugby/football). What other ways of throwing can children devise (for example, stand with the back to direction of throw and throw over the head)? A medicine ball can also be used for this activity.

(10) **Throwing the Wellie** (or Plimsoll). Old Wellingtons can make novel throwing implements and will be thrown with enthusiasm. Allow experiments with different techniques – two-handed, over arm, round arm.

(11) **Sling the quoit**. Round arm throwing holding the quoit 'discus style' can help discus throwing later. With children of five to 11 simple team competitions can be devised, or there can be competition within small groups.

(12) **Gain Ground** – use a medicine ball (or football for younger children). Play across one-third of a netball court with four to five a side, or larger numbers (six to eight) on, say, the penalty area of a football pitch. The aim is to throw the ball over the opponents' line. Each team takes it in turn to have a throw – the next team throws from where they stop the ball.

*Measuring*

If competitions are simple, markers are sufficient (squares of white card on long nails, old badminton shuttlecocks weighted with Plasticine and so on). If more accurate measurement is required for recording (as for incentive schemes) it helps if the throwing area is marked with arcs every 10 metres. For speed of measuring, measure from the nearest arc. A long tape pegged at the throwing point can also be used for speedy measuring to within one metre. With practice, with either method, an estimate to within half a metre is quite possible, and as the points on incentive schemes rise in half to one metre steps, this is sufficient; it also allows many more throws to be taken.

For true accuracy, measure from point of landing to the throwing point. It may also help speedy measuring if a child holds the tape at the throwing point and the teacher takes the tape to the landing point. This will produce accuracy to within 5 centimetres which is enough at this stage.

*General strength training*

In addition to specific throwing activities, all athletes will benefit from strength training. (See Appendix I, Glossary of Strength Exercises, pages 109–13.)

**Superstars** A simple competition is to total the number of press ups, sit ups, squat thrusts and squat jumps performed in 20 to 30 seconds. Step ups, dips, chins and cossack dancing may also be added. A team or partner competition can easily be worked out from this.

**Partner work** Piggy-back races, broken wheelbarrow, indian arm wrestling, push/pull activities can all be used. Numerous others abound but are outside the scope of this book. These activities are included as samples of what might be done and indicate the range of activities that can benefit athletes.

**Circuit training** The simplest form of circuit training is for children to work for, say, 30 seconds at an activity, and then, after a 30-second rest, move round to the next activity. A sample circuit involving a range of muscle groups is:

1 Step ups on to a bench.
2 Sit ups.
3 Squat thrusts.
4 Squat jumps or vertical jumps to touch wall just above stretched height.
5 Chin or pull ups on beam or bar (allow the feet to touch the floor after each one – that is, perform the pull ups with a jump).
6 Shuttle runs.
7 Press ups.

A card indicating the activity should be at each activity area. This list is capable of wide variations and developments, but this sample involves hardly any equipment. As the children progress, targets can be set to be achieved in the 30 seconds. For example, three grades of circuit targets are set for each exercise. The step ups might be 20, 30 and 40. Children are allocated their grade according to ability, or all start at grade 1 and build up. When a circuit at grade 1 has been achieved, attempt grade 2. It is possible to set individual targets for each child at each exercise, but this is time-consuming.

**Weight training** The best advice on weight training for eight to 13s is – DON'T DO IT.

# SECTION II

# Class Lessons

## Warm up

It is recommended that all P.E. lessons begin with some warming up activities, and athletics is no exception to this. The phrase 'warm up' is something of a misnomer, as the activity is necessary even on the hottest day. The children need to perform activities that stretch their joints and muscles as well as stimulate their circulation. A third important benefit is the mental preparation for the coming effort. Senior athletes purposely use the warm up to build up their concentration, but with young children it is also used to eliminate any over-excitement and to accustom them to obeying orders and moving as and when instructed – in fact, to get them in the correct frame of mind.

For formal athletics with experienced older athletes, the warm up would take a minimum of 20 minutes and consist of jogging, mobility exercises and further running of increasing intensity or, for jumpers and throwers, run up practice, technique drills and so on. Clearly this is not practical in a school situation, nor is it as necessary. However, some warm up should take place, and the chasing games (tag) or reaction games (O'Grady) mentioned earlier (page 10) are very suitable. As athletes grow in experience, the warm up will develop.

## A INTRODUCING ATHLETICS

The approach to P.E. varies from school to school. Some schools have class games lessons, others year games. Some have a syllabus for each year involving a block of lessons devoted to various aspects of P.E., others have a very flexible approach. Whether a block of athletics is imposed or each teacher is free to devote a few lessons to athletics, the approach can be the same.

The block, or group, of lessons must have clearly defined *aims* and *objectives*: what is to be taught, how and why. Much of this should be clear from the place P.E. has within the school curriculum and the place athletics has within the specific syllabus. In the construction of the syllabus thought will have been given to the *time*, *facilities* and *equipment* available.

Before embarking on the block of lessons, the skills to be taught must be understood and the approach must be planned. It is not effective to decide, 'It's a nice day – we'll do some athletics.'

When the block has finished, there must be some *evaluation*. Were the aims and objectives fulfilled? If not, what was the reason? Do the aims need reappraising? Does the P.E. curriculum need reappraising?

## Non-standard events (much of the Ten-Step and some Five-Star events)

These events are the easiest to introduce and organise. They give children an introduction to athletics and provide an opportunity for experience in timing and measuring.

The approach will vary according to the children, their age and experience. It is suggested later that older children may be enlisted to help with eight- to nine-year-olds. Their presence should enable rapid progress, but asuming a class of ten-year-olds were attempting the Ten-Step scheme (see pages 77–9) for the first time, progress could be:

### Lesson 1 (indoors) (Figure 23, page 56)

Class of 30 in six groups of five. Time 30 minutes. Two groups perform:

(a)  standing long jump;
(b)  standing three spring jumps.
The remaining four groups perform simple skill circuit activities from, for example, netball shoot, hockey dribble slalom, hockey shoot at a narrow goal, football dribble slalom,

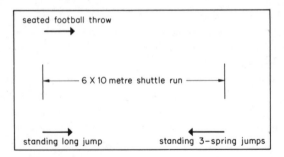

Figure 23   *Ten-Step Award*
*Two possible indoor layouts (badminton court size)*

*(a) 15 metre hop, standing triple jump, object pick up and slalom run can all be used indoors as alternatives to the events suggested (plus standing football throw).*

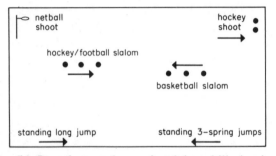

*(b) Introductory lesson involving skill circuit activities as well as athletics.*

basketball dribble slalom and many other possibilities, all of which are easy to explain and attempt.

The jumps groups should measure, but not record, their performance – there could be a simple competition to find the best in each group. The teacher's time would be devoted more to these groups until he/she was satisfied the measuring was satisfactory. Always insist on two children measuring – this helps accuracy, reduces guessing and maintains involvement.

The skill circuit groups should have a stop watch, stop clock, or digital watch and count, for example, how many netball goals (set posts at lower than competition height) are scored in 20 seconds. Thus the group are gaining timing practice.

After three minutes, groups change round until everyone has experienced each activity and has timed and measured.

## Lesson 2 (indoors)

As above, but introduce a further skill, reading a watch, by timing how long it takes to score two goals (or any set number). It is advisable to set a time limit (say 20 or 30 seconds for the two goals) or one child could still be trying to score after 3 or 4 minutes.

Possibly introduce the recording of results (or leave until Lesson 3).

## Lesson 3 (outdoors) (Figure 24, page 58)

Introduce new events (see Figure 24). Children will be familiar with the two jumps and the slalom idea so teachers can concentrate on the very new events, seated soccer throw, 15 metre hop and shuttle run. If desired, five groups of six children would mean that only two new events are included.

Subsequent lessons can add new events in place of established ones whenever the teacher wishes, to maintain variety.

## Preliminary class work on timing, measuring and recording

Simple measuring of objects varying from pencils to cupboards should be part of normal maths work. Children must be made aware of the different ways in which metric measurements are noted on rulers, small tapes, long tapes and metre sticks. To measure the same object with each of these soon establishes understanding. Some children will happily record three or four widely different results and not realise anything is wrong. The task of noting results neatly and clearly is also valuable training. Timing can be encouraged by simple timing games. The class should divide into groups according to the number of watches/clocks available. Each child, in turn, is the timekeeper for the group. The teacher calls 'Go' and then 'Stop'. The result from each group is compared to the teacher's time. This can be developed by groups timing a child performing a skill such as throwing and catching a ball five times. Children can be timed walking round the hall or playground, and many other varied activities will spring to mind.

As with measuring, children must be aware of stop watches with 30 second sweeps, 60 second sweeps, watches timing in tenths and fifths, and digital watches (often timing in hundredths).

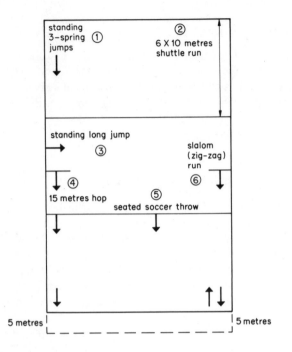

Figure 24   *Ten-Step Award*
            *A possible outdoor layout (netball court)*

            *Alternatives*
            *Area 1 or 2   High jump (on to crash mats)*
            *            Standing triple jump (hop, step, jump)*
            *Area 4, 5, 6 Standing soccer throw*
            *            Object pick up*
            *            Compass run*

            *By extending the court 5 metres, a circuit of 100 metres
            makes a 400 metre walk or 800 metre run possible.
            Depending on the proximity of classrooms and protective
            fences, some throwing of cricket/rounders balls may be
            possible (most children throw less than 30 metres).*

# B FORMAL ATHLETICS

To go on to a field and expect to teach 30 children to long jump, perform a relay, or even sprint start, without planning, is to invite chaos. Each athletic event should be treated as a new sport or game – which it often is.

The foundation, once again, lies in the normal P.E. lesson – for example, jumping activities, reaction games, throwing skills with play balls.

Progress made beyond the introductory stage will vary. Some events are easy to handle with a whole class (middle distance) and others impossible (high jump). The solution is to divide the class into groups (say 15 from a class of 30 children). One group is instructed in the athletic skill requiring most of the teacher's attention, while the other three groups of five are designated to other athletic events (such as long jump – free practice, but measuring and recording results), or another sport (such as continuous cricket). It is assumed that sufficient time has been devoted to these to enable children to participate with slight supervision. Many Ten-Step or skill circuit activities come into this category. Depending on the time available, the groups rotate during the lesson or over a series of lessons.

## Suggested lesson plan, illustrating this approach

Class of 30 10- to 11-year-olds. Time 30 minutes.
(a) Warm up activity 5 minutes (see page 54)
(b) Divide class into group A – 15
　　　　　　　　　　　　group B – three groups of five
　　Group A are instructed on long jump skills (see page 32), three to five stride approach, high take-off from side of pit. Develop to three strides take-off from board.
　　Group B perform: standing long jump (see Assignment cards, 2, below);
　　　　　　　　　　　seated (or standing) football throw;
　　　　　　　　　　　6 x 10 metre shuttle run (see Assignment cards, 1, below).
　　Every three to four minutes visit group B and rotate their activities then change groups A and B.

# C ASSIGNMENT CARDS

If using a skill circuit approach, or small groups as above, teachers may want to prepare *assignment cards* detailing the simple skill or activity to be performed. The rules and instructions for timing/measuring/recording should be clearly noted. If a hall or playground is used, it will help if areas are marked. A netball court with a line down the centre (longways) has six clearly defined areas, a badminton court has five (four service areas plus centre section). For example:

1 *Shuttle run* (6 x 10 metres)
  (1) Start – toes behind the line.
  (2) After each 10 metres, one foot must touch the line before turning.
  (3) Starting commands: 'On your marks', 'Set', 'Go'.
  (4) Record the time to the nearest tenth of a second.

7  6 × 10 metres shuttle run, run individually.

2 *Standing long jump*
  (1) Start – toes behind the line.
  (2) After landing – walk forward, do not sit or step back.
  (3) Measure to the landing point nearest the starting line, usually the heels.
  (4) Record the distance to the nearest centimetre.

3 *10 metre power hop* (use area 4 of the netball court)
  (1) Stand on the back line of the netball court.
  (2) Hop, on the same foot, to the first line parallel to the back line, counting hops.
  (3) Repeat using the other foot.
  (4) Repeat trying to use fewer hops.
  (5) Devise a simple team or pairs competition.

4 *Throwing the rugby ball* (use football pitch penalty area)
  (1) Practise throwing the rugby ball in several ways, such as:
    (a) One handed (try left and right hands);
    (b) Two handed facing forwards (underarm and over-head);
    (c) Two handed facing sideways;
    (d) Two handed facing backwards.
  (2) Devise a simple team competition using one or more ways of throwing.

# D EVENTS FOR EACH YEAR GROUP

The following is a suggested list of *formal* athletics events that may be attempted.Teachers, of course, may wish to add or delete from the list according to their needs and facilities.

## Eight-year-olds

60 metre sprint, shuttle relays, steady running (one to two laps of the football pitch), long jump (measure from the point of take off), hurdles (stage 1), throwing (tennis balls).

## Nine-year-olds

As above, but add baton relays for enjoyment (little technical instruction). Long jump – take off from board later in season. Hurdles – low obstacles. High jump – early stages.

## Ten- and 11-year-olds

All events except shot, discus, javelin and triple jump.

## Twelve- to 13-year-olds

All events on incentive schemes (but see Section IV, Competition, page 89, for distances for running).

NOTE 1   Baton relays – some L.E.As (or Areas/Divisions of L.E.As) include baton relays for eight- to nine-year-olds. If this is the case then, of course, teach baton changing. However, it is doubtful if the standard by the age of eleven will be much improved unless a great deal of time is spent, and, unless a school is very fortunate, time is a commodity in short supply.

2   As well as the formal events, conditioning activities and Ten-Step or Five-Star events that are not formal athletics events should be covered.

# E SUGGESTED LESSONS

## (i) Indoor lessons – school hall

In a hall of badminton court size, the following can be covered:

*Running*
Starting practice – distance 10 metres maximum
Reaction games
Shuttle runs/relays
Early relay practices with batons

*Jumping*
Standing long jump
Standing triple jump
Standing three bounds
Hopping (15 metre hop may be just possible)
Long jump from three strides on to crash mat or gym mats
High jump from three strides (see Figure 25)

*Throwing* (play balls)
Throw and catch
Throw at a target
Seated and standing football throw
Medicine ball throw

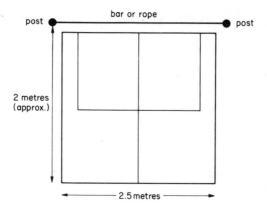

Figure 25 *(a) Indoor high jump landing area (if crash mats are not available)*

*For 3-stride approach – low level scissors jump practice*

*Two piles of (approx.) 2 × 1.25 metre mats, each pile 3 to 4 mats thick plus one on top to ensure no gap.*

*Similar constructions are possible with 2 × 1 metre mats, or a combination of sizes.*

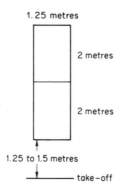

*(b) Indoor long jump landing area*

*For 3-stride approach – emphasis on technique not distance*

*Two piles of mats, 3 mats per pile. Ensure that mats are pushed together after each jump. This allows a 3 metre jump with 2 metres in hand for pitching forward.*

## (ii) Indoor lessons – sports hall athletics

If a school has a sports hall or large gymnasium, then as well as the events and activities given above a greater range is possible.

A branch of indoor athletics, 'Sports Hall Athletics', was introduced in 1978 and has proved very popular. The events covered are sprints, hurdles, relays, middle distance, standing long jump, standing triple jump, vertical jump and shot put. These can all be incorporated in a hall 25 metres long. Special equipment is available* which is obviously advantageous, but lacking of the equipment should not prevent some adaptations.

The running events are assisted by 'Reversaboards' which are angled at 50° to the end walls to assist turning. Thus any number of lengths can be run.

The standing long jump uses a 'Metromat', a mat on a solid base with a measuring scale up to 4 metres. For the triple jump, five mats joined with velcro are used. The fifth mat is graduated up to 3 metres. The jumpers choose, according to ability, which starting line on the other four mats to use.

The vertical jump measures the height above the jumper's stretched height that can be reached by a standing jump. This means that short children can compete against tall ones at no disadvantage. A measuring board can be lowered or raised to meet the tips of the jumper's stretched fingers.

For shot putting, a correct weight shot is used, but one constructed for indoor use and having a shock-absorbing plastic cover to avoid damage to the hall floor.

In competition, over 300 children have competed in the course of an afternoon, so for class lessons a group of 30 could cover several events in 45 minutes. The Five-Star award tables now cover the indoor 'Sports Hall Athletics' events and can provide an alternative incentive to straight competition.

---

* For details contact Eveque Leisure Equipment Ltd, Dock Road, Northwich, Cheshire, CW9 5HJ.

# (iii) Playground lesson – netball court

As for indoors *plus*:

*Running*
Starts – up to 20 metres
Shuttle relays over 15 to 20 metres
Baton relays – see relays section (pages 13–20)

*Jumps*
High jump – full event if on to crash mats
Long jump – full event if pit is alongside playground

*Throws*
Standing football throw
Tennis ball throw, possibly cricket/rounders ball throw depending on safety
Shot put, using 'indoor' shot
Medicine ball throw

# (iv) Wet days – What do I do if it is raining?

(1) If a hall or gymnasium is available refer to E, Suggested Lessons, page 62–4, for indoor athletics.
(2) If the children have to remain in a classroom, the disappointment at missing a games lesson (and, if it is a generally wet day, missing mid-morning and lunch break playtime) will result in some resentment if normal lessons are substituted. As alternatives therefore:
(a) refer to the section on timing activities (page 57) and perhaps add competitions on estimating of distances.
(b) invent a quiz on rules for competition and procedures for timing, measuring and jumping.
(c) use video tapes. The increasing availability of video recorders in schools should be utilised and a selection of athletics or general sports films should be available. If film has been taken of the children competing or practising then this is even better. Apart from the instructional aspect, children love watching themselves on film.

## (v) Suggested six-week block of athletics (Easter to Whitsun)

Ten-year-olds, one hour per week (assumption made that preliminary activities have been carried out)
1 Sprints and shuttle relays
2 Long jump – early stages
3 Throws, middle distance time trials
4 Sprints, high jump
5 Baton relays
6 Sprint races, long jump

At each session, some groups will be working on Ten-Step/skill circuit/continuous cricket and so on, while instruction is given to other athletes. Groups should then change round.


## F  GUIDELINES

As with any aspect of P.E., each lesson or group of lessons should have aims and objectives. With young children, enjoyment and purposeful activity should be two aims; the third should be the purpose of the skill or skills being taught. The initial experience should stress the recreational aspect of athletics, not the competitive. Exhortations such as 'Nice guys come last', 'Who remembers who came second', 'Hate your opponents', 'Winning is what it's about' may (only may) have a place in the phrase book of potential Olympic champions, but should have no place in a school P.E. philosophy. Of course, children will enjoy competing, it is a great incentive and any normal child prefers winning to losing, but the old Olympic ideal can surely be taught in schools if nowhere else.

### (i) Attitudes

The attitude of the teacher to a sport, if it is a wrong attitude, will either rub off on to the child and produce a fiercely competitive child who cannot accept fair defeat, or crush a child's enjoyment and enthusiasm. Too often a teacher, through enthusiasm, will go beyond teaching basic skills and try to impose an advanced skill, often in the process becoming fault-orientated. An athlete may perform 90% of a skill correctly – the coach/teacher seizes on the incorrect 10% and ignores the correct points. By all means correct faults (how else can a child learn?), but *encourage* by pointing out, and praising, what was correct, and this often includes praising effort as well as correcting errors. If a child is being pushed to perform a skill beyond his/her present ability, he/she will concentrate on the advanced skill and forget the basics. A notable example is the hundreds of school children attempting a hitch-kick long jump. Only a mere handful can jump high enough and far enough to have the time to perform the skill correctly. (In fact, many international class women do not use this technique.) The majority just twiddle their feet in the air in the vague, and vain, hope it will improve their jump. So anxious are they that they neglect the controlled run up and take off which are the keys to good jumping. A former National Coach, Wilf Paish, has stated: 'Children are not interested in the world of hitch-kicks and straddle jumps, they are interested in how far and how fast. It is this that motivates them.'

Most sophisticated skills 'as seen on the telly' demand a mature, fit athlete to perform them. To expect a young child to perform like an experienced adult athlete is comparable to expecting back somersaults from a nine-year-old gymnast who has just passed B.A.G.A. Award 4.

Too many school teachers feel that because they do not understand advanced skills they cannot teach athletics. Nothing could be further from the true situation. Purely by organising children's natural enthusiasm to run, jump and throw, a great deal can be achieved. With an understanding of only the basic skills teachers can be pleasantly surprised at the successful results.

## (ii) Organisation

Whatever the aims and objectives, they will not be achieved without *planning*. A few minutes thought to revise and *note* what is to be done and what equipment is needed can make all the difference to the success of a lesson. The overall planning of the group of lessons, the part played by athletics as part of the P.E. curriculum and P.E. as part of the school curriculum, would ideally be planned by the P.E. post holder in consultation with the headteacher. Whoever is responsible would do well to heed the advice in *Movement: Physical Education in the Primary Years* (D.E.S., 1972).

'Teachers must make sure that the content of the athletics programme and the methods of presentation are not discouraging or inappropriate to primary children, especially to the younger and less gifted. All too quickly that which is child-like and a stimulating medium of growth for every child may become something which is essentially adult in its nature, with the result that progress is inhibited for all but a few precociously able or specially gifted children.

Wide ranging activities practised throughout the primary years can provide the experience and skill which are essential preliminaries to the more stylised athletic events.'

## (iii)  Clothing and hygiene

The headteacher or P.E. post holder will also be responsible for setting the procedure for clothing and hygiene. In most junior schools, showers are rare, though most middle or secondary schools have them. Wherever possible, children should be encouraged (a) to change completely for P.E. (that is, no classroom clothing should be worn) and (b) to shower after P.E.

With regard to clothing, footwear used for outdoor lessons should not be used for indoor ones. In cold weather, tracksuits or extra (old) jumpers worn over P.E. kit are essential, and are useful even in summer.

Whatever decisions are taken about clothing and showers, children *and parents* must be told of the rules, and if the reasons are explained, cooperation is much more likely because the rules will seem sensible and in the interests of the children.

### Spikes

It is financially impractical to provide spikes for all children, nor is it even possible to obtain very small spikes. Undoubtably, the school team will benefit from wearing spikes. Simple time trials will show the advantage on grass. Should the grass be wet or just damp, or the race be on a cinder track, then the advantage is even greater. (Some areas may decide that, because all children cannot have spikes then no one should wear them at District Championships.)

# (iv) Key facts and progression

When explaining a new skill or activity, it is all too easy to confuse children in a welter of explanation. *Keep it simple* (K.I.S.S. – 'Keep it simple, stupid') by means of *key facts* – the essential points expressed in a few words. Progress from this brief explanation to a *demonstration* (by teacher or child), then let the children *experience* the skill. They will then be more ready to listen to further advice – and may even have their own valuable suggestions for improvement.

*Develop* the skill by simple stages. Do not rush, but continually reinforce and repeat key facts by advising and encouraging at all times.

A point worth noting is that adults perform many skills automatically and sometimes their method may not be the method they are trying to teach. Therefore when setting down your key facts, try the skills yourself – but *left-handed* (assuming you are right-handed). This forces you really to concentrate on basics and also puts you in the position of an uncoordinated child and helps your understanding of his/her problems. In addition, it will also help you to demonstrate to a left-handed child.

# (v) Timing

Timing is often inaccurate in schools due to the lack of a good starting pistol (.38 or .45), the inaccuracy of the stop watches, and the inexperience of the timekeepers.

As a .38 starting pistol costs about £50, and cartridges about 10p each, plus the cost of a licence, few junior schools can completely remedy the first problem. However, a .22 pistol is within a reasonable budget and can reduce the margin of error.

A simple check on the accuracy of a stop watch is to start it on a time signal from the 'Speaking Clock' and stop it again on a signal 20–30 minutes later. This gives a clear indication of the degree of error. Two seconds over 30 minutes is only .1 in one and a half minutes – a margin of error acceptable for normal school purposes. If the error is greater, the watch can be adjusted by a local jeweller. Watches should be checked each year, but many are never checked from the time of purchase. All too often it is assumed that if they work they must be correct.

## Care of watches

(a) Never leave a watch wound up or the timing will be affected. Ideally leave it ticking and wind up before use. This is difficult to enforce if several teachers, and many children, handle the watches, so it is always advisable to run the watch for a few minutes before using it.

(b) Do not permit the watch to be swung around, nor for the athletes to time themselves carrying the watch. Any such times must be disregarded.

(c) Digital watches are now very good value for money and easier for children to use.

Inexperience of the timekeepers can easily be cured – by experience and thought! The latter is essential; five years of making the same mistakes is not what is meant by experience.

The timekeeper should start the watch simultaneously with the flash and smoke from the gun. If the timekeeper is 50 metres from the starter and starts the watch on a sound (of gun, whistle, clapper-board, or shout, whichever is being used as a starting signal), the sound reaches the athletes well before the timekeeper. If a .22 is used, there is some flash and a little smoke, and the reactions to these may be a little slow. The advantage gained by the athlete is about .2 second. If a starting pistol is not used, two methods may help the timekeepers. First the starter should drop his hand (holding a flag or handkerchief) as he shouts 'Go'. This is not easy to coordinate. The second method involves the position of the starter. Ideally the starter should stand a few metres *ahead* of the athletes and to the side. However, if the starter stands about 15 metres ahead of the athletes and the timekeepers stand 15–20 metres from the finish, the gap (over a 50 metre race) between them is 15–20 metres and so the athletes will hear the signal at the same time as the timekeepers. The timekeepers must be able to *walk* to the finish in order to time the race. Timekeepers must watch the starter closely, not the athletes. A good starter raises his gun (or hand) just before saying 'Set'. As he does this, the timekeeper holds the watch steady and takes up the first pressure (presses gently) on the starting button, and when the flash or other signal is seen, presses firmly without jerking. At the finish, the timekeeper watches the athletes until they are 10–15 metres away from the line, then watches the line. He or she does not anticipate the finish but stops the watch when the athlete's torso (not head, arms or feet) crosses the line. It is essential to hold the watch steady without jerking.

## How do I cope with timing several runners?

First, do not try to time too many. If the teacher is the only timekeeper, run the children in groups of three, time the first and third (using two watches or a watch with a 'split' function (that can take two times) and estimate the second athlete as follows. If runner number 1 is timed at 8.5 (over 50 metres) and runner 3 at 8.9, where was runner 2? If close to 1 (just daylight between) then give 8.6, if no daylight give the same time. If close to 3 give 8.8 or 8.9 on the same basis. If mid-way between give 8.7. Qualified timekeepers will probably be horrified at such rule-of-thumb timing, but even they sometimes have to estimate if one time is missed and there are insufficient timekeepers to cover every athlete with two watches. If the athletes are graded by ability, there should not be a large gap between them. For middle distance races, one watch, kept running, can be used for several athletes. If the watch is held on the clipboard so the timekeeper can see the runners and the watch at the same time, the time to the nearest second can then be recorded. An alternative is to pair off the runners. Number 1s of each pair run in the first race and as they cross the line the timekeeper calls out the time – for example, 3 minutes 14 seconds, 3.15, 3.18, and so on, and number 2s remember their partner's time. Number 2s run in the second race, number 1s checking their time. If children are used to assist in the timing (perhaps using digital watches with a stop watch function), then use the children to time 2 and 4, the teacher taking 1 and 3, using the most capable child on 4. The teacher should amend any dubious times. The best position from which to time is standing *back* from the finishing line – and ideally above ground level. The latter is impractical for practices, but staging blocks can be used for inter-school matches.

## (vi) Judging

The best view is obtained as for timing – back and high. For further suggestions, see Section IV, Competition, sprints (page 96). It is worth encouraging children to wear a variety of tops as even six bizarre tee-shirts or football jerseys are preferable to six black leotards or white singlets. This enables a judge to recall that Red beat Black, then came Green (which is easier than 'Paul, then John, then, er, what's-his-name').

**Judging jumps** (see Section IV, Competition, pages 100–3)

Again – stand back. If children are used, work in pairs to double check, and maintain involvement.

**Judging throws** (see Section IV, Competition, pages 103–6)

Children detailed to retrieve balls stand beyond the 50 metre line and move to retrieve only when told. One judge is needed to note over-stepping of the throwing line, but the next child to throw can fulfil this role.

Best view of landing is from the side, *not* from in front. The judge should watch the ball land, then ignore it, keeping the eyes on the landing point. If two or more judges are available, spread them out (for example, for ten-year-old boys, one judge stands at 25 metres, the other at 40 metres). As the ball is in the air the judge moves towards the estimated landing point, thus as the ball lands at least one judge, possibly both, will be almost level (within 2 to 3 metres) of the landing point, and should be able to move in to the precise spot the ball touched. The judge must *never* be concerned with the retrieval of the ball; always have others to perform this function.

Young children should not judge discus or javelin.

## (vii) Equipment

Even in times of comparative affluence, few schools could buy whatever P.E. equipment they needed. In the present austere times the budget has to stretch and the following ideas may help.

*Batons*
Cut up old broom handles, cut broken shinty sticks or cricket stumps; tape two or three old (chipped or splintered) rulers together.

*Hurdles*
Scrounge unserviceable hurdles (not capable of being raised above 61 centimetres) from secondary schools. Make up hurdles by using garden canes, fixed with bulldog clips to squeezy bottles filled with sand, or by placing canes across plastic cones.

*Starting pistol*
(a) Cap guns can be almost as loud as .22.
(b) Make a clapper-board from two pieces of wood about 30 centimetres long and 15 centimetres wide by 1 centimetre thick. Join with a hinge and fit two handles.
(c) Purchase a 'clapper' starting unit.

*Timing*
Stop clocks are cheaper than stop watches (although a minimum of two stop watches should be available). Allow children to use their own digital watches with stop watch function.

*Jumping*
For high jump, use a weighted rope (see page 38) or an elastic 'bar' as marketed by Kay-Metzler. For high jump stands, use multi-purpose stands which can double as stool ball bases.

*Measuring*
Use dressmakers' tapes (1.5–2 metres) for standing jumps, or Imperial yard sticks cut to 50 centimetres. Paint distances alongside pit or on playground.

*Landing mats*
Do not throw away mats no longer suitable for indoor P.E.; they can be used for landing in standing long jump in the playground or for the surrounds of a crash mat (high jump).

*Throws*
Tennis ball cores are very cheap (about 5p each). Scrounge old tennis balls from local tennis clubs and old cricket balls from cricket clubs.

Rubber discoi are cheaper than wood and metal ones, and quite suitable for practice.

Dowelling rods with taped or hose grips can serve as introductory javelins.

Old rubber balls can be filled with sand or even cement to make weighted 'shots' or javelin training implements.

# SECTION III

# Incentive schemes

The objective of an incentive scheme is to provide athletes with progressive, graded challenges in all activities. The star athlete has to work to meet the next challenge rather than relax as top dog. In any school the best athlete in a year is not always outstanding when compared with children in other schools. A good incentive scheme can help prevent the athlete (and the teacher) getting a false impression of his/her ability. Average or below average ability children, with little or no chance of representing their school or house, or of ever winning a race, can be transformed from no hopers and losers (and therefore potential drop-outs) into enthusiastic triers. To strive for, and gain, a realistic objective is as much success as winning. If a child can enjoy working to improve his/her performance and perhaps receive a badge or certificate to mark that achievement, then the benefit to that child is much greater than simply the enjoyment and satisfaction of sports participation. Maturity in approach to life in general is a real possibility. Success through effort at some goal often triggers off further effort in other spheres, particularly with the less able or less confident child.

Five possible incentive schemes can be used. Teachers can decide which one or combination of schemes can best suit the physical education curriculum in their school. The five possibilities are: the *Five-Star Award Scheme*; the *Ten-Step Award Scheme*; *English Schools A.A. 'Milk in Action' Award Scheme*; *Thistle Award Scheme* (Scotland); and a *School Standards Scheme*, tailored specifically to individual school needs.

# A FIVE-STAR AWARD SCHEME

This scheme was developed from an almost unique and highly successful school standards scheme, devised by Alan Launder, when at Dr Challoner's School, Chesham. The scheme was developed and launched through the drive and enthusiasm of Tom McNab (then a national coach), initially in Southern England in 1967 and then nationally, and the scoring tables were compiled by Dave Couling. The scheme involves children being tested from a full range of athletic events and scoring points according to their performance. The best three events (at least one run and one jump or throw) are totalled and the child obtains a one, two, three, four or five-star award. Such is the grading that a one-star award is within the reach of almost every child who is prepared to practise, and yet only a few will reach the five-star. The age range starts with second year juniors and goes up to sixth form secondary pupils. There is no limit to the number of attempts a child may make to improve a performance, and once one level is reached the motivation exists to strive for the next. Pentathlete (five events) and Decathlete (ten events) awards are also possible provided at least one run, one jump and one throw are included in the events.

Certificates are available free of charge and badges may be purchased. Once a child moves up an age group, the challenge becomes harder to achieve the same level of award. A ten-year-old boy may achieve a three-star with 80 points but will need 110 points to gain a three-star as an 11-year-old. This needs an improvement of, for example, 2.90 metres to 3.30 metres in the long jump and similar progress in two other events. Thus the scheme is graded within each group and between age groups.

Several events are included specifically for under 12-year-olds which take note of restricted facilities which exist in many areas. The scheme can be operated by a school with only a netball court sized playground available and no field, although obviously the choice of events will be very restricted. Events specifically for under 12s are 50 and 75 metre sprints, 55 metre hurdles, 50 metre skipping, throwing the cricket/rounders ball and 1000 metre walk. Further events that do not require a field are standing long jump, standing triple jump, 70 metre sprint with two turns, 210 metre sprint with six turns and vertical jump (a measure of height of jump above stretched height). These have been included to cover sports hall athletics (see Section II, Class Lessons, page 64). In addition, high jump, long jump, 100, 800, and 1500 metre sprints and perhaps others can be added from the general list which includes all the possible secondary events. Details of the scheme (notes and scoring tables) are available from A.A.A. (Five-Star), Francis House, Francis Street, London, SW1P 1DL.

# Five-Star Cross-Country Running Award

This scheme was introduced in 1982 and is unique in that it is the only incentive scheme to cover cross-country. Moreover, children gather the bulk of their points by training.

Briefly, children accumulate points in three ways.

## 1 Training

For each training session (regardless of length) over a ten-week period, six points are scored up to a maximum of 110 points, which includes a bonus of ten points for reaching the magical 100 point figure.

## 2 Competition

This may be within a class or teaching group. A sliding scale allocates points according to the position finished as a percentage of the competitors for example, 25 points for first, second or third, 15 points for top 50% down to five points just for finishing.

## 3 Time trial

Held over distances ranging from 800 metres to 2000 metres (girls) and 1000 metres to 3000 metres (boys). Points are scored according to time up to 50 points. More than one trial can be attempted.

According to the points accumulated, children may gain awards according to those points and their age group. Take, for example, two 11-year-old boys, A and B.

| | |
|---|---|
| *A* trains once a week for ten weeks (6 × 10) | 60 |
| Finishes 45th out of 50 in a race | 10 |
| Runs 1500 metres time trial in nine minutes | 7 |
| Gains a two-star award for | 77 points |

| | |
|---|---|
| *B* trains 18 times in ten weeks (6 × 18) + ten bonus | 110 (max) |
| Finishes 20th out of 50 in a race | 15 |
| Runs 1500 metres time trial in eight minutes | 16 |
| Gains a four-star award for | 141 points |

The strong emphasis on accumulating points by training cannot be praised too highly. Over and again, this book has emphasised the need for a background of training before racing middle-distance or cross-country, and this scheme gives an admirable incentive to train.

The scheme may be operated as a cross-country club, meeting as an out of school activity, or can operate during school games lessons. A run of 1000 to 1500 metres at the start or finish of a lesson would not take up much time. A class or group list prepared for the training runs can very quickly be marked; most names could be marked off during the run. The course does not have to be the same every time. Even if the school field has to be used, try to plan some variety.

Details of the award, including notes for guidance are available from Mr F.A. Keen, 'Westways', Upper Tadmarton, near Banbury, Oxon.

# B TEN-STEP AWARD SCHEME

This scheme was devised by Tom McNab with the plight of junior schools with restricted facilities very much in mind. Over half the events (ten out of 19) can be performed in a small playground and at least seven can be performed in the school hall. Several others can, with a little ingenuity, also be adapted for a restricted area.

The scheme was introduced in 1979 in the South of England and has expanded steadily since. Many concepts are the same as those of the Five-Star scheme, but it covers eight-year-olds as well as nine-plus years, and embraces a wider ability range, particularly at the lower end, in some events (for example, 50 metres and high jump) where children may be excluded from the Five-Star charts.

Thus, whereas the Five-Star scheme is excellent for the school club – those of above average ability and enthusiasm – it is restricted in use as a class activity, particularly with eight- and nine-year-olds. On the other hand, the Ten-Step scheme fits in admirably with a class lesson but perhaps does not stretch the most able ten-to-12-year-old.

The children score points according to their performance and then total their best five events (one run, one jump, one throw, plus any other two). Certificates are available free and badges may be purchased. The points required for any level do not change from age group to age group, thus a nine-year-old gaining a four step may progress, perhaps, to six or seven as a ten-year-old and aim for nine or ten as an 11-year-old.

The events in the Ten-Step scheme are listed below. To try all events would be confusing, therefore it is advisable to restrict events to those suitable to a school's facilities. Start the first years with a limited number and gradually increase the events available as children progress through the school, thus maintaining variety and interest.

The suggested age groups are put alongside the events; these are a personal choice and are suggestions only.

| *Running* | *Jumping* | *Throwing* |
|---|---|---|
| 50m (8+) | Standing long | Seated soccer |
| 75m (10+) | jump (8+) | throw (8+) |
| 50m skip (8+) | Standing triple | Standing soccer |
| Shuttle (6 × 10) (8+) | jump (10+) | throw (10+) |
| Compass (10+) | Three spring | Cricket/rounders |
| Slalom (8+) | jumps (10+) | ball (8+) |
| 40m hurdles (10+) | 15m hop (8+) | |
| 800m (9+) | High jump (9+) | |
| 400m walk (8+) | Long jump (9+) | |
| Object pick-up | | |
| race (8+) | | |

Thus:

Eight-year-olds have a choice from five running events, three jumping and two throws.

Nine-year-olds have a choice from seven running events, five jumping and two throws.

Ten-year-olds have a choice from ten running events, six jumping and three throws.

Eleven- and 12-year-olds have a choice from ten running events, six jumping and three throws.

It must be emphasised that teachers can introduce *any* of the events to *any* age group, but it is recommended that there is some selection, otherwise children will be confused.

Further details (notes and charts) are available from Mr A.J. Kendall, 10 Squires Lane, London, N3, or S.C.A.A.A. (Ten-Step), Francis House, Francis Street, London, SW1P 1DL.


# C ENGLISH SCHOOLS A.A. 'MILK IN ACTION' AWARD SCHEME

This scheme was introduced in 1982 and was resoundingly popular with 300,000 badges being sold.

The scheme covers primary and secondary schools with three levels of award for primary schools and five for secondary schools.

The three levels common to both age groups are Gold, Silver and Bronze, with Merit and Credit being lower levels for the older pupils.

All basic events are covered in five groups:

|          | *Primary*                                                  | *Secondary*                                        |
| -------- | ---------------------------------------------------------- | -------------------------------------------------- |
| Sprints  | 40m (under 8), 60m (under 10) 80m (under 11)               | 100m, 200m, 400m                                   |
| Distance | 800m                                                       | 800m, 1500m, 3000m, steeplechase★                  |
| Hurdles  | 55m (height 50–61 cm, 5 flights and spaced to suit child)  | 70m to 400m according to group                     |
| Throws   | Cricket/rounders ball                                      | Shot, discus, javelin, hammer★                     |
| Jumps    | High jump, long jump                                       | High jump, long jump, triple jump,★ pole vault★    |

★ Not for girls

Examples of primary standards are:

| Boys | 80m | *Long jump* | *Cricket ball* | 800m |
|------|-----|-------------|----------------|------|
| Gold | 11.3 sec. | 3.60m | 38m | 3 min. 10 sec. |
| Silver | 13.0 sec. | 2.80m | 25m | 3 min. 25 sec. |
| Bronze | 15.0 sec. | 2.20m | 15m | 3 min. 50 sec. |

Thus a young able primary school child is likely to start by achieving a Bronze award and gradually progressing to a Gold award by the age of 11.

The less able 11-year-old is still likely to be able to gain the Bronze award in at least one group of events and so achieve some success.

Once a child has achieved the required level in any event in a group he/she can buy a badge for that group (for example, 3m 60cm in the long jump gains a Gold *jumps* badge).

The badges cost 40p (1983); 5p of this is returned at the end of the year to the school and 5p to the County Schools A.A.

With simple tables and no points totalling needed, the scheme is very easy to run – a major advantage for hard-pressed teachers. The fact that a child can gain a badge in just one group does not mean that specialisation is encouraged, and teachers should ensure that children attempt a range of events and aim to gain awards in several groups.

One unique feature has been added to this scheme: special amendments have been made to the tables to enable children with physical or mental handicaps to participate and receive awards. With the current trend towards educating children with special needs in normal schools this has relevance to all teachers, not just those in special schools.

Full details of the scheme, including the name and address of the agent for each county, may be obtained from the Secretary of the English Schools A.A., Mr Neal Dickinson, 'Davidiane', 26 Coniscliffe Road, Stanley, Co. Durham.

# D THISTLE AWARD SCHEME (SCOTLAND)

This scheme was started in 1971 and was devised by Frank Dick, now (1983) Director of Coaching for the British Amateur Athletic Board.

The scoring of points according to performance is similar to the Five-Star Scheme, but the scheme is unusual in two respects. First, the age range is not just for children but extends from under nines to over 44s – so the teacher can have a go, too! A second unusual point is the method of gaining an award. A points target is set for each age group and if this is reached with two events (one track, one field) then a Gold award is achieved. If the target is reached with three events, a Silver is achieved, if with four events, a Bronze, and if with six events (two track, two field and two track or field) then a Blue award is achieved.

Badges and certificates are available for each category. Examples of the scoring are as follows:

| *Boy A (age 11)* | | | *Boy B (age 11)* | |
|---|---|---|---|---|
| Long jump | 4.04m | 14 | 2.95m | 6 |
| High jump | 1.30m | 13 | 90cm | 4 |
| Shot | (2.72 kg/6 lb)6m | 11 | 3.50m | 3 |
| 60m | 8.7 sec. | 15 | 9.6 sec. | 7 |
| 800m | 2 min. 52 sec. | 15 | 3 min. 16 sec. | 8 |
| 1500m | 6 min. 12 sec. | 12 | 7 min. 40 sec. | 2 |

Boy A has achieved a Silver award, reaching the 30 point standard in three events. He just missed the Gold (29 points in two). His 60 metres and 800 metres which each scored 15 points are both track events, so his 14 points for the long jump had to score.

Boy B reached 30 points in six events and gains a Blue award.

The range of events is a full one and the throwing events use light implements for younger ages, including the slingball which is a weight with a handle. Unfortunately, it is rarely seen outside Scotland; it is an excellent implement for teaching basic throwing techniques in discus, hammer and javelin.

An inter-school competition is also organised through the scheme. Schools score four points for each Gold award, three for Silver, two for Bronze and one for Blue, and the total is divided by the number of pupils on roll. There are six categories of school depending on size and type.

Full details of the scheme including notes for guidance are available from Thistle Awards, 18 Ainslie Place, Edinburgh, EH3 6AU.

# E  SCHOOL STANDARDS

The previous four schemes are sophisticated forms of school standards. Teachers who use them may still wish to have a standards scheme tailored to the needs of their school.

When constructing a scheme, various questions need to be considered:

1 What is the objective of the scheme?
2 What is the incentive to the children?
3 What events are to be covered?
4 Is the scheme to have one scale for all years, or one for each year?
5 Are all children to participate or is it selective?
6 How many grades are needed?
7 How should the grades be constructed?

## 1  Objectives

(i) The scheme may be narrow – to provide points for 'also-rans' on sports day.
(ii) It may be wide – to provide each child with realistic pro-gressive goals.

## 2  Incentive to the children

(i)   Points on sports day.
(ii)  Points for house team throughout the year.
(iii) Certificates/badges specifically designed for the school.

## 3  Events

A starting point should be a sprint, middle-distance, long jump, high jump and cricket ball or rounders ball throw.

To this list could be added any of those events covered by the other incentive schemes. Additionally, if the same cross-country course is used for each year, standard times can be set for this, as in the Five-Star Cross-Country scheme. Not all events need to be standardized for each age group.

## 4 Scales

A wide ranging scale, covering from 2 metres to 4 metres in the long jump, or 60 centimetres to one metre 40 centimetres in the high jump, could cover all children in the school but would need perhaps ten intermediate points or even more. One scale for each year may be easier to construct and administer – for example, eight-year-olds: 2 metres long jump up to 3 metres with three to five intermediate points.

## 5 Are all to participate?

Certainly this ought to be the case. Thus the lowest grade must be attainable by the less able child who makes an effort.

## 6 Grades

(i) A five point scale gives greater flexibility – for example, grade 1 – rarely achieved, only by the very best; grade 2 – school representative standard; grade 3 – average child; grade 4 – below average; grade 5 – less able but a trier.
(ii) A three point scale would cover 1, 3 and 5 of the above, with perhaps grade 1 being made a little easier and 5 harder.

## 7 How to construct

(i) Use Five-Star tables (or another scheme's tables). If 60 points is the grade 1 for 11-year-olds, then sub-divide down to ten points for grade 5, for eight-year-olds, 30 points down to one point. These can either be taken as they are or used as a starting point and adjusted in the light of previous performances.
(ii) Test every child in every event, or one class in each year to form a base, and then adjust in the light of performances from previous years when necessary.

For the eight to ten-year-olds, little difference will be found between boys and girls, but above that age a slightly higher level for boys is necessary.

## Which scheme is best?

Only the teacher can decide. How much time available for athletics in lesson and out of school, how much support from colleagues, and what facilities are available, are only three of the
variables that must be considered. The Ten-Step is perhaps
better for a class lesson, the Five-Star, Thistle Award and
English Schools Schemes for a school club. The individual
scheme is ideal but *very* time-consuming to prepare initially.
The English Schools Scheme could very easily slot in in place
of a School Standard scheme and save a great deal of work. It
has to be your choice for your school which scheme – or combination of scheme – will be operated.

# F TESTING AND RECORDING FOR THE INCENTIVE SCHEMES

It is permissible for children to test each other and all marks
are acceptable if the teacher in charge is satisfied. Of course,
children first need to be taught how to use a stop-watch and
tape measure and the different means of registering that they
may have. Within the school may be stop-watches with 30 seconds and 60 seconds per revolution, reading in tenths or fifths.
One tape measure may record in metres and centimetres (i.e.,
3m 60), the other may be in metres (3.6), with metre sticks
recording millimetres. As part of the science and maths
activities, children should become familiar with timing and
measuring. Of course they will make mistakes – they make
mistakes in every sphere of education – but they will not learn
without the experience of trying. Of course, some children will
cheat – just as they will copy in class. Fortunately they are not
very sophisticated cheats at this age and magical one metre
improvements in a long jump soon sound warning bells to the
teacher. Cheating and inaccurate measuring can be checked
(but not eradicated) by careful selection of groups. During the
season the teacher should ensure that he or she times and measures each child, thus setting an accurate figure against which
doubtful performances can be cross-checked. By observing
each group timing/measuring, an opinion can soon be formed
as to their accuracy.

8 Slalom run, showing children timing and recording.

If the first time a class time/measure, the performances are noted but not recorded, then many first-time errors will not matter. The standard and the accuracy will be higher next time.

Ten-year-olds and above can become very good judges and timekeepers, but obviously younger children, in general, will lack the ability and experience, although some nine-year-olds can be very capable.

To help with the timing and measuring, it is often possible to borrow one or two experienced older children. They are often those whose class work will not suffer from the occasional half an hour's absence and the social gain is also very much a plus.

Do you accept performances achieved outside the school? This must be a matter for individual decision. Certainly the performance must be verified by the scoutmaster/youth leader or official of the local athletics club. It would clearly be foolish to refuse to accept a time recorded on a cinder track, timed by a qualified timekeeper; equally a time achieved in doubtful circumstances should not be accepted. Always bear in mind that a child may mishear, or misinterpret a time or performance. An estimate given to a child, 'That was about "x" ', will be regarded as an actual time; furthermore, many children will regard 14.0 seconds as being a correct rendering of any time between 14.0 and 14.99 – they are all 14 seconds something and the 'something' is ignored.

How often should the teacher test? As mentioned earlier, the first occasion performances are timed or measured should be regarded as a practice, but it is important to have performances recorded fairly soon to gain interest and provide motivation for further improvement. However, if every session is devoted to testing, little instruction can take place. There is no reason why one group should not be measuring their own long jumps while the teacher gives baton relay instructions to another.

## Recording

The Five-Star, English Schools and Thistle schemes provide wall charts for class/group recording, and similar charts can be drawn up on graph paper, thus providing a focal point for athletics notices and maintaining interest. Performances should be recorded in pencil to facilitate inserting improvements during the season, which should be done regularly.

Result cards are commercially available, but multi purpose sheets can easily be drawn up. The covers of old desk diaries make useful boards to which the result sheets can be clipped to facilitate writing out of doors.

| Name | 15 metres | standing long jump | cricket ball | slalom run | 6 X 10 metres shuttle |
|------|-----------|--------------------|--------------|------------|-----------------------|
| - - - - - - - - - | | | | | |
| - - - - - - - | | | | | |
| - - - - - - - | | | | | |
| - - - - - - - | | | | | |
| - - - - - - - | | | | | |
| - - - - - - - | | | | | |
| | 50 metres | 800 metres | 3-spring jumps | cricket / rounders ball | long jump |
| - - - - - - - - - | | | | | |
| - - - - - - - - | | | | | |
| - - - - - - - | | | | | |
| - - - - - - - | | | | | |
| - - - - - - - | | | | | |
| - - - - - - - | | | | | |
| - - - - - - - | | | | | |

Figure 26   *Ten-Step Group Result/Recording Sheet*

Children also expect teachers to have an encyclopaedic knowledge of the score charts ('What do I get for a 3.25 metres long jump?', and so on ). If the score charts are mounted on card or board and covered with a protective plastic sheet, they can be readily available at practices and can be consulted by the children.

# SECTION IV

# Competition

## A  SCHOOL CLUB

The selection of children to participate in athletics out of school hours will of course depend on the time and facilities available, and the assistance of colleagues. Within reason, all children who wish to participate sensibly should be encouraged to do so. However, it may be prudent to restrict some practices to certain age groups – for example, a separate session for eight-to-nine-year-olds, or to the school team squad only – especially just before competitions such as the District Sports.

All the award schemes are suited to a school club, although the Ten-Step is possibly better for eight-to-nine-year-olds. It is hoped that basic skill teaching has already taken place in class P.E. or games lessons, but this cannot be assumed, nor can it be assumed that no further basic instruction is needed: It is the keener, and generally more able, athletes who attend these sessions and skill teaching to this group can be most rewarding; they are hungry to learn and enthusiastic to work.

The incentive schemes should not dominate the school club. At least half of each session, or half of the sessions, should be devoted to skills or conditioning rather than test, test, test. In the early part of the season the skills and conditioning should have even greater emphasis.

The presentation of certificates and badges should be made an occasion, not just be passed out in class. Depending on the time available, either one main presentation at the end of term or one before half term and a second at the end of term could be arranged. The latter gives an incentive to strive for the next stage during the second half of the term. The presentation can be made at an assembly and, if possible, could be made by a school governor, P.T.A. official, secondary school teacher (P.E.) or, if available, a locals sports personality. The sense of occasion elevates the status of even a one-star certificate.

# B SPORTS DAY

## What sort of occasion is it?

Is it a major spectacle before parents and governors? Or is it a casual affair on a suitable warm afternoon? Whichever option is chosen, the day must be organised and have prior planning. Even if it is supposedly a casual, informal affair, someone must know what is going to happen and what is needed.

## Who takes part?

There should be only one answer – every child who is capable of doing so. Even those unable to compete due to medical reasons – long or short term – can have a job and thus be part of the day.

## What events are held?

These can be sub-divided into formal and informal (fun) events. Both have a part in a junior school Sports Day.

### Formal events

*Sprints*
60–200 metres (under 12s should not race more than 100 metres) depending on age. Some form of selection may be necessary before the day, or heats and finals held on the day, but this may prolong the programme. If heats are held prior to sports day, those eliminated should still be able to enter informal events.

*Jumps*
High jump, long jump.

*Throwing the cricket/rounders ball*
The inclusion of these events may be governed by facilities,

time and availability of judges. They can take place if necessary at a subsidiary time, perhaps with the heats of the sprints, or spread out over two or three lunch times. Points, prizes or other rewards given on sports day should also be awarded to events held at other times.

It is, perhaps, advisable to restrict the throws and jumps to ten-year-olds and over. If a suitable area is available, the throwing of cricket or rounders or even tennis balls can be a spectacular event on sports day. Coloured cones or flags can mark each competitor's throw and give a boost to an event that is all too often pushed into the background. Middle schools catering for 12- and 13-year-olds may also wish to include shot, discus, javelin and triple jump.

*Relays*
These make an exciting finale to sports day. A suggestion is:
Eight- and nine-year-olds – 4 × 40m (or 6–8 × 40m) shuttle relay
Ten- and 11-year-olds      – 4 × 75m baton relay
Twelve- and 13-year-olds – 4 × 100m baton relay
Teams can be inter-house, inter-class, or inter-tutor group.

*Middle distance*
A 600 metres or 800 metres race for ten-year-olds and above (1500 metres for 12-to-13-year-olds) will generate excitement. This means that unless the children are adequately prepared the sense of occasion could cause them to race off over-quickly and the shouts of encouragement may force a child to continue to the point of physical distress. It is certainly likely to cause an emotional reaction, especially from girls, at the finish which must be distinguished from genuine distress.

The tendency to collapse dramatically at the end should be eradicated at practice sessions. Often children can be miraculously cured by a warning that if they collapse again they will not be permitted to race or run a time trial until they have completed three to four weeks' more training. With experience comes the realisation that staying on their feet and walking does promote a more rapid recovery.

**Informal (novelty or fun) races** (particularly for younger children)

These, especially sack races or obstacle races, can be as physically demanding as formal events, but can involve children not blessed with rugged physiques or natural speed. Events requiring coordination rather than speed and strength – for example, egg and spoon or slow bicycle races – can give success to the also-rans in the 80 metres. Even those who come last in these are not so discouraged because of the fun element. The novelty features usually include some luck aspect and thus the races are not foregone conclusions.

The number of informal races are countless, the limitations being equipment and time. An occasional longer event such as a slow bicycle race can aid the recorders to catch up with the results, but too many events of this type can prolong the day too much.

## Who decides the events?

This can be done by the person in charge of P.E. or a consensus of the staff (whose cooperation is essential). Perhaps the P.E. specialist could decide the formal events and each member of staff chooses the two or three novelty races for their class or tutor group.

## When should Sports Day be held?

It can serve as an early season incentive to get athletes moving and to aid in casting a wide selection net for the District Sports, but it *must not* mark the end of athletics for 80% of the children.

It can serve as an end-of-term outlet for pent-up energy. The needs of the school dictate the date and purpose.

## What officials are needed?

*Adults* are needed – the children trained to help with incentive schemes are competing. Staff are supervising their classes. Thus the services of the P.T.A. can be called upon, or fifth or sixth formers from local schools who may be ex-pupils. Staff may agree to share responsibilities such as three staff supervising five classes, thus releasing two staff to act as officials.

*Starter*
Using .22 pistol or whistle.

*Marshal*
One or two, to get children to the start at the right time for the right event.

*Judges*
At least three for sprints and two for novelty races.

*Recorders*
If names of winners are needed and points are awarded.

*Prize distributors*
If prizes, medals, certificates, sweets or such are to be given (governors fulfil this role excellently).

*Equipment stewards*
(For race equipment) can be provided by children.

*Announcer*
Chairman of the P.T.A. is usually a good choice.

If the head teacher and teacher in charge of P.E. can stroll around during Sports Day, keeping a benevolent eye on things without a specific job to do, then it has been well organised.

## Preparation

Start thinking well ahead as to date, events, need for loud speakers, first aid, and so on.

The organiser should put him/herself in the position of each group of participants in turn – staff, children, parents, guests, officials. Assume it is their first Sports Day. What are their actions throughout the day? How do they know what to do? What information do they need? Who gives it to them? What equipment do they need? Where will they obtain it? Where do they sit? Obtain refreshments? Find access to toilets?

For example, parents – how do they know the date and time? Where do they sit when they arrive? How do they know what is going on? (Programmes to be prepared and sold, announcer appointed.) Can they obtain refreshments and use toilets? When and where do they collect their child at the end?

Each set of questions provokes thought and ensures small details are not overlooked. It is often these minor details that cause problems if overlooked and give an impression of lack of organisation.

Do not assume that everyone remembers the procedure from last year, or remembers instructions given at a staff meeting. A sheet of written information is a worthwhile aid to a smooth day.

As soon as the day is over, commit to writing points for debate or improvement next year.

# C INTER-SCHOOL COMPETITION

In most areas there is some form of district championships or a major inter-schools competition. This does not affect the need for or value of further inter-school matches. If a main competition exists, then a match against another school gives competitive experience to your team, and if there is no main competition it is an excellent alternative incentive.

## Who should compete?

As many as administratively possible should compete. If four sprinters from each school contest each race (four age groups, boys and girls), 32 children are involved in this alone. It is not essential to evolve a complex scoring system, needing several judges and recorders; the first two from each school could score: for example, 4 points for first, 3 points for second, 2 points for third, and 1 point for fourth. Even if a school finishes first, second, third and fourth, only the first and second athletes score points (4 + 3 points). The children do not need to know the scoring system.

If possible, two relay teams per age group can involve a further 32 children. Thus without middle distance, jumps, or throws, 64 children per school can be involved. For a middle distance race for ten-to-11-year-olds (600 metres or 800 metres), four to six per school could run – again with only the first two from each school scoring. A school with only three runners is not at a disadvantage with this system. With jumping and throwing events the time factor will probably restrict the competitors to three per school, perhaps combining ten-to-11 and 11-to-12-year-olds. The structure needs to be flexible to allow maximum participation and yet be simple to administer.

# D   OUTSIDE CLUBS, SECONDARY SCHOOL LINKS, COACHING AND OFFICIATING

The minimum age for participation under A.A.A.'s and W.A.A.A.'s rules is 11 years old. Although some clubs do accept young children below this age it is debatable whether it is a sound policy in general.

The circumstances of a particular area may be such as to make an under-11 policy a useful community service. Ideally a club catering for under-11s needs to be separate from a club for older athletes. In most inter-club competitions an average ability fourth-year junior will be outclassed, but many well organised clubs arrange graded competition within the club and their officials and coaches are as concerned for the young athletes' welfare as the teachers are.

If possible, contact local clubs, visit their training sessions and assess what they can provide. Many clubs allow youngsters to attend for a few weeks before joining, which is a sensible policy. By attending a few training sessions, teachers are better able to assess the relative ability of the children in their schools and form an opinion on the services, supervision and competence of the club.

## Further incentives

Further incentives can be given to the children in conventional forms by displaying photographs or posters of international athletes, ensuring an adequate library of athletics books and maintaining up-to-date progress charts. If a school is within range of main athletics centres such as Crystal Palace, Birmingham, Cwmbran, or Gateshead, then visits to major meetings will be very popular. The Coca-Cola and Talbot Games at Crystal Palace always draw excited crowds of school children, without the problems of large crowds at football fixtures.

## Secondary school links

The liaison between junior and secondary school teachers (and first/middle/senior schools) is most useful in all subjects, not just in P.E. A keen athlete will settle down more quickly if the secondary teacher can say, 'Oh yes, I know about your athletics. I'm looking forward to seeing you run/jump/throw' as appropriate. If the P.E. staff at secondary schools assist on Sports Day, issue certificates in assembly and so on, all the children moving up to their schools will benefit from seeing a familiar face during the first few worrying days.

It may be possible for an inter-school match to take place on the secondary school track, utilising fifth or sixth formers as judges – an excellent form of community service.

## Qualifying as a coach

The U.K. Coaching Scheme has three grades, Senior Coach, Club Coach and Assistant Club Coach. The last qualification is aimed at coaches working with large numbers of young children and is ideal for teachers. The details of forthcoming courses locally can be obtained from the area coaching secretary – address via A.A.A. or W.A.A.A. Blackpool Easter School and Loughborough Summer School both organise residential courses, highly recommended and enjoyable!

The College of Preceptors has just (late 1983) introduced a new qualification, 'Associate of the College of Preceptors (Athletics in Education)'.

## Qualifying as an official

Each County Association (address from A.A.A. or W.A.A.A.) administers its own officials tests and organises courses of instruction. It is possible to qualify as a timekeeper, starter, starter's assistant (marksman), track judge, and field judge; the knowledge gained will be most useful in school athletics.

## E RULES FOR COMPETITION AND ADVICE ON JUDGING AND MEASURING

### Sprints

#### Distances

Recommended distances were mentioned earlier in this section (page 89). Girls under 15 may not (under W.A.A.A. laws) race at distances between 200 metres and 600 metres.

## The start

1 Fingers and toes, in contact with the ground, must be behind (not on) the starting line.

2 If any runner starts before the signal, the race must be re-called and the athlete responsible warned. A second false start by the same athlete should result in disqualification.

NOTE With very young children, this may need modifying. At all levels it is not a false start if an athlete overbalances without attempting to 'beat the gun'. Many young children do over-balance and need reminding to hold steady. When dealing in the eight to ten age group it may be worth the teacher concerned deciding not to disqualify so readily, but any child who persistently tries to gain an unfair advantage should eventually be disqualified.

3 An athlete who runs out of lane and gains an advantage, or hinders another runner, should be disqualified. With very young children it may be sufficient to move the offender down one or two places in the finishing order. Do not assume that very young children know the purpose of the white lines.

## Judging

Few people, unless they are experienced judges, can accurately judge and remember several places, particularly with all competitors in black leotards or white tee-shirts, a normal school situation. Therefore, if there is only one judge, do not attempt to place beyond the first three or four and restrict the numbers to perhaps five or six per race. If several judges are available – even children – ask each judge to select a different place, i.e., one judges first place, another second and so on. After a close finish this can result in the same child being selected for two positions and another not being selected. To overcome this, ask each judge to remember any athlete just beaten by, or just beating, his or her choice. If one adult is assisted by children the adult concentrates on close finishes. If in doubt, give a tie – this keeps everyone happy. At meetings where a result is important, then sufficient adult judges should be available, although it is advisable to have one chief judge overseeing the close finishes.

The best position for judging (and timing) is *not* right on top of the finishing post but standing well back, preferably on a raised platform.

For important competitions, competitors should wear numbers, front and back, securely pinned, and contrasting vests or tee-shirts. The judges should then be asked to select the finishing order of all the runners and only if they have insufficient experience to do this should the methods suggested above be used.

## Sprint relays

### Rules

1 Dropping a baton is *not* a reason for disqualification. However, the runner who drops the baton must pick it up and must not obstruct other teams (for example, by going into another lane) while so doing. It is when the wrong runner retrieves the baton or obstructs that disqualification will occur.
2 Even after passing the baton, if a runner steps out of lane and obstructs another team, his team may be disqualified.
3 Batons must be exchanged within the 20 metre zone. This rule has recently been clarified. The baton must be within the take-over zone when it is in the grasp of the outgoing runner only. Thus, the outgoing runner may have his feet outside the zone but his hand just inside at the moment of transfer.
4 If teams have to run heats and finals, the team order may be changed but not the team except through illness or injury. The meeting referee should always be consulted before such a change.
5 It is not permissible for anyone (child, teacher, or parent) to instruct the outgoing runner when to start running, although he or she may assist in marking the check mark.
6 With older children the acceleration zone may be used. The athlete may commence the run from this zone but the baton must be exchanged as in rule 3.

## Hurdles

### Distances

The standard distances recommended by the English Schools A.A. for under-13s are:

    70m – 8 hurdles at 68cm, 11m to the first hurdle, 7m between hurdles

75m – 8 hurdles at 68cm, 11.5m to the first hurdle, 7.5m
   between hurdles

For younger children, the incentive schemes suggest shorter
distances and lower hurdles with the spacing adjusted to suit
the children. Reference should be made to the appropriate
scheme for full details. As a guide, when spacing to suit
athletes, a run of 9 to 10 metres to the first hurdle and 5 to 6
metres between hurdles would suit most and could provide a
starting point.

## Rules

Athletes must clear all hurdles and must not run round the
sides, push hurdles over by hand, or deliberately knock hurdles over with the feet. Accidental hitting with the feet is permissible.

# Middle distance track races
# (up to 3000 metres)

800 metres and 1500 metres are the most usual, both being
possible for incentive schemes. 600 metres is also a suitable
distance – it fits nicely on to a 300 metre track. Races beyond
these distances should not be attempted by under-11s.

By now it should be quite clear that children should not
attempt to race until they have had sufficient preparation. The
1500 metres in particular should not be raced, but is better run
as a time trial if for the Five-Star award. Perhaps two or three
children of similar ability may run together, but a large field
would cause several to set off too fast.

A general emphasis on time trials is a sound one. Children
will still race but, regardless of where they finish, can derive
pleasure from a personal best time. Among the ranks of those
who rarely, if ever, win will be children with little sprinting or
jumping or general sports ability but who have stamina and
*enjoy* running. What a tragedy if they were to be denied the
pleasure in a most healthy of pastimes by either an over-
protective attitude ('it is far too far for you to run') or an over-
competitive attitude.

It cannot be stressed too strongly that children should not

race competitively without adequate training. One does not enter a child in a swimming gala who can barely swim the required distance.

## Rules

1 For distances beyond 400 metres there is no 'Set' command. 'On your marks' is followed (when all are steady) by 'Go'.
2 No lanes are used, but athletes must not obstruct another athlete when moving to the inside lane, or when moving out to overtake. Emphasise, when overtaking, get clear before cutting in.

At the start, remind athletes not to rush to the inside but to move in easily. It is better to run a lane wide for a few yards rather than crash to the inside.

## Cross-country and fun runs

A fairly flat parkland course is ideal, but hard to find; thus utilising the school field is usually necessary. Ten-year-olds who have had a background of training, can cope with 1500 to 2000 metres.

If large numbers are participating, preliminary organisation is essential.
1 The course must be clearly marked and explained, and preferably marshalled by non-participants as a double check.
2 The finish must be clearly evident with a funnel (see Figure 27 page 100), marked with flags and ropes, to channel the finishers away from the line.
3 Make out small squares of card (three centimetres square) numbered from one up to the expected number of runners plus ten for safety. These can then be issued in order to each finisher.
4 Delegate non-participants to collect these numbers and record the names. One recorder to each ten to twelve finishers will avoid anyone being swamped with names.

At all times, in all practices and races, stress to children that they are not to collapse at the finish. If one goes down, the rest will surely follow with Oscar-winning performances. Athletes who are exhausted will recover more quickly by staying on their feet and walking; most are *far* from exhaustion point.

A simple team race can be worked out from a cross-country

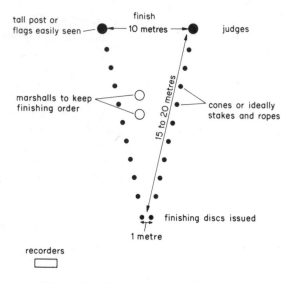

Figure 27  *Cross-country finishing funnel*

run. If the scores from each team are added together (first – 1 point, second – 2 points, third – 3 points, and so on). Team A may have 1, 5, 7, 8, 11 = 32 points. Team B – 2, 3, 6, 9, 10 = 30 points. Team C – 4, 12, 13, 14, 15 = 58 points. Team B, with the lowest score is the winner. If teams tie, the one with their last scorer home ahead of their rivals' last scorer is the winner. The problem of uneven numbers in teams is resolved by scoring the first five or six (or more) from each team. Leave each team with one or two spares, just in case someone drops out. These non-scorers can, in fact, help their team by beating scorers from other teams, thus making their opponents total higher.

# Long jump and triple jump

## Rules

1 *No jumps* – a no jump occurs when any part of the foot is over the front edge (near the pit) of the board. It is *not* a no jump if the take-off is before the board.
2 *Number of jumps* – in most school competitions three jumps each is sufficient but up to six are permitted. Ideally, all have three jumps and the best six have a further three.

3 *Tie* – if two or more have the same distance, the second best jump decides the tie. If that is equal, the third best and so on.
4 In the triple jump, competitors may elect which take-off board to use to enable the jump phase to land in the pit.
5 In the triple jump the 'sleeping leg' (that is, the non-active leg) must not touch the ground during the hop or step phase.

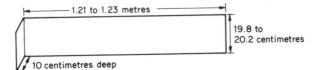

Figure 28 *Long jump board (and triple jump)*

*The board must be white, and flush with the ground.*

## Measuring

For accuracy measurement should be from the rearmost point of landing (usually the heels, but the athlete may fall or step back) to where the tape crosses the front edge of the take-off board (edge nearest pit). For practices where distances are for information and interest, not complete accuracy, it speeds up the practice if the tape is pegged level with the front edge of the board and run alongside the pit. Thus a fairly accurate assessment (within ten centimetres) can be made immediately. If the pit has a concrete or tarmac surround, the distances could be marked every 10 centimetres (the numbers only need to be put down for the metres and either 50 centimetres or 20, 40, 60 and 80 centimetres).

The best view for judging no jumps and for marking the landing point is to the side, not right on top. At least one judge should judge no jumps and at least one the landing point. Two or more to each job aids accuracy and maintains involvement.

For accuracy, the pit should be raked level after each jump.

# High jump

## Rules and competition

1 A bar should be used. The pegs for the bar should point in to the bar, not towards the pit and *never* towards the approach.

2 The landing area must be large enough to ensure children do not land on the ground. 4m × 2.5m should suffice but 5m × 4m is ideal. If sand is used in the landing area, it must be *dug* not just raked regularly. If crash mats are used, they must be secured together so no gaps occur.

3 During competition, athletes do not have to jump at each height. They are eliminated after three successive failures. For example, if an athlete clears 95 centimetres but fails once at 1 metre, he/she does not have to jump a second or third time at 1 metre (but would normally do so). If the child fails again at 1.05 metres, he/she has now had two successive failures and a second failure at 1.05 metres would be a third successive failure. He/she would then be out of the competition with a clearance at 95 centimetres. However, most children will try to jump at each height until successful, unless they are called away to a race. (This takes priority, and the bar may be raised in their absence.)

If two or more clear the same height, the winner is the one with fewest jumps at the height cleared. If this still leaves a tie, the one with fewest failures in total is the winner. If this still leaves a tie, competitors share the place unless it concerns first place, in which case they have one more attempt at the lower height failed and then lower and raise the bar 1cm at a time until one clears a height the other fails at. (This rule is a recent amendment.)

4 Athletes may run up and stop without jumping, provided they do not touch the ground or landing area beyond the posts.

5 Two 'old wives' tales' need to be scotched:
   (a) it is not a clearance because an athlete has got off the landing area or out of the pit before the bar falls,
   (b) it is *not* a failure if the athlete makes two abortive run-ups.

Both these seem to have arisen from rule of thumb guides. If an athlete touches the bar, lands, gets up, walks back and the bar is still shaking the judges have to decide how long to wait before steadying the bar – especially if the wind is blowing, it may shake for ever. It would be reasonable to steady the bar when the athlete has returned calmly and the next jumper is ready. Do not encourage frantic scrambling out of the pit. With regard to abortive run ups, a competitor may not make *unreasonable* delay before taking a jump. Sometimes the reluctance to jump can become contagious and restricting jumpers to only one 'refusal' may speed up competitions within a school but should *not* be enforced in inter-school competition.

6 Jumps must be from *one foot*. Take-off from two feet in a gymnastics type dive is not permitted.

# Throws

1 Each competitor may have from three to six throws; usually all have three throws and the best six a further three.

2 In the event of two athletes throwing the same distance, the second best distance shall decide the position. If that is also equal, the third best decides and so on.

3 The measuring point of each implement is the rearmost point of landing, which must be within the defined throwing area.

4 Competitors must not touch the throwing line or ground beyond during the course of the throw or *afterwards*. In the *shot* and *discus* competitors may touch the side of the stop board or inside rim of the circle but not the top of the rim or board. Having thrown, they must leave the circle under control via the rear half of the circle.

In the *javelin* and *cricket/rounders ball*, competitors having thrown and the implement having landed, they must retire from behind the throwing line or its extension.

5 *Shot*

The shot must be pushed from the neck and must not be withdrawn prior to throwing.

6 *Javelin*

(a) No unorthodox methods are allowed (for example, rotational slinging).

(b) The javelin must land tip first but does *not* have to stick in.

## Weights of implements

The English Schools A.A. recommend the following specifications for under-13s:

|          | *Boys*           | *Girls*          |
|----------|------------------|------------------|
| Shot     | 3.25 or 2.72kg   | 2.72kg (6 lb)    |
| Discus   | .75kg or 1kg     | .75kg            |
| Javelin  | 400g             | 400g             |

## Throwing areas

*Shot*
The shot should be from a concrete circle 2.135 metres (7 feet) diameter. The front edge should have a curved stop board 1.22 metres long and 10 centimetres high by 11.4 centimetres thick.

The shot should land in a 40° sector (recently changed from 45°).

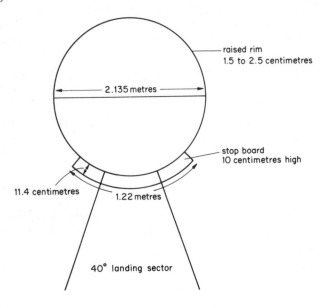

Figure 29   *(a) Shot put circle*

*Discus*
The discus circle should be 2.5 metres (8 feet) diameter. There is no stop board and the landing sector has recently been reduced from 45° to 40°.

*Javelin*
The throwing line should be 4 metres long and curved from a 8 metre diameter arc. The landing sector is much tighter – 29°.

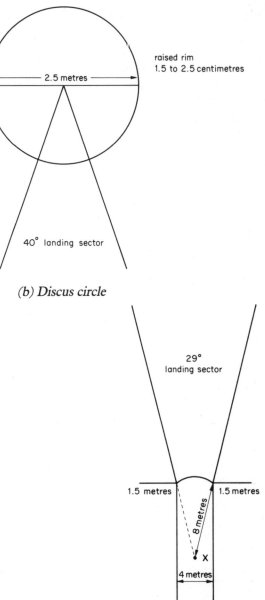

raised rim
1.5 to 2.5 centimetres

2.5 metres

40° landing sector

*(b) Discus circle*

29° landing sector

1.5 metres    1.5 metres

8 metres

X

4 metres

Figure 30  *Javelin run up*

*For true accuracy the tape measure should stretch from the landing point through to point X and be read off where it crosses the inside (thrower's side) of the throwing line.*

*Cricket/rounders ball*
No set landing sector is specified but the javelin sector is a
sound guide.

The above rules are shortened and simplified versions of the
full A.A.A.s/W.A.A.A.s rules and reference should always be
made to these. However, nothing has been omitted that would
prevent fair competition.

# Bibliography

British Amateur Athletic Board official publications
(obtainable from B.A.A.B./A.A.A. Sales Centre, 5 Church Road,
Great Bookham, Leatherhead, Surrey, KT23 3PN)
*But First – Basic Work for Coaches and Teachers* by F.W. Dick

Separate event books include:
*Shot Putting*
*Discus Throwing*
*Javelin*
*High Jump*
*Long Jump*
*Triple Jump*
*Sprinting and Relay Racing*
*How to Teach the Throws*
*How to Teach the Jumps*
*How to Teach Track Events*
*How to Organise an Athletics Meeting*
*How to Judge Track Events*
*How to Judge Field Events*
*Starting and Timekeeping*

Also available:
*Wall Charts* (set of six: High Jump, Long Jump, Hurdles, Shot, Sprints
and Relays)
*A.A.A. Handbook* (including Rules for Competition)
*I.A.A.F. Basic Coaching Manual*
*W.A.A.A. Rules for Competition*

Further recommended books

ANTHONY, D. (1982) *Field Athletics*. (Batsford)
COULING, D. (1980) *Athletics: A handbook for teachers*. (Hale)
JARVER, J. (1983) *Athletics for Young Beginners*. (A.H. Reed/Rigby
International)
JOHNSON, C. (1982) *Field Athletics* (new edition). (E.P. Group)
KINCAID, D. and COLES, P.S. (1973–7) *Sports and Games* (SCIENCE IN A
TOPIC series). (Hulton)
LE MASURIER, J. and WATTS, D. (1980) *Athletics: Track Events*. (A. and C.
Black)
LE MASURIER, J. and WATTS, D. (1982) *Athletics: Field Events*. (A. and C.
Black)
McNAB, T. (1980) *Athletics*. (Hodder and Stoughton: Knight Books)

McNAB, T.(1970) *Modern Schools Athletics*. (Hodder and Stoughton: out of print)

PAISH, W. (1976) *Track and Field Athletics*. (Lepus Books)

PAYNE, H. and PAYNE, R. (1976) *Athletics: Throwing*. (Pelham)

TANCRED, P. and CARTER, C.A. (1980) *Athletic Throwing*. (Faber)

WATTS, D. (1974) *Tackle Athletics this Way*. (Stanley Paul)

WATTS, D. (1976) *Athletics: Jumping and Vaulting*. (Pelham)

WHITEHEAD, N. (1978) *Track Athletics* (new edition). (E.P. Group) *Know the Game* series – *Athletics*.

Department of Education and Science (D.E.S.) (1972) *Movement: Physical Education in the Primary Years*. (H.M.S.O.)

Films available on hire from:

British Olympic Film Library, Pottery Lane, London, W11 4LZ

I.A.A.F., 162 Upper Richmond Road, London, SW15

Guardian Royal Exchange Films, Guild Sound and Vision, Peterborough.

Army Kinema Corporation, Chalfont Grove, Chalfont St Giles, Bucks. (for the 1936 Olympic film, 'Festival of Nations')

Institut Francais, 15 Queensberry Place, London, SW7 (for an inspirational athletics film, 'Summer Rendezvous')

Magazines

*Athletics Weekly*, 344 High Street, Rochester, Kent, ME1 1DT

*Athlete's World* (monthly), Peterson House, North Bank, Berryhill Industrial Estate, Droitwich, Worcs., WR9 9BL

*Athletics Coach*, B.A.A.B., 9 Moorfield Drive, Halesowen, West Midlands, B63 3TG

# Appendix I
## Glossary of Strength Exercises

## INDIVIDUAL EXERCISES

### 1 Press ups

Stage 1 (for beginners)
Kneel on the floor and extend body forward with the upper legs and back in a straight line. The arms should be straight, supporting the body. Lower the body by bending the elbows to 90° and then straighten.
Target in 30 seconds: 20 = Fair (F), 25 = Good (G), 30 = Excellent (Ex).
Stage 2
As above, but with the toes on the floor so that the legs and back are in a straight line. This is called the 'front support position'.
Target for 30 seconds: as in Stage 1.

### 2 Sit ups

There are many variations. Try these:
(a) From lying on the back, sit up to hug the knees.
(b) From lying on the back, sit up to hug alternate knees.
Target in 30 seconds: (a)  14 = F, 18 = G, 22 = Ex.
(b)  16 = F, 20 = G, 25 = Ex.

# 3  Squat thrusts

From front support position (Press ups, Stage 2), bring the
knees forward to the elbows and then thrust back.
Target in 30 seconds: 25 = F, 30 = G, 35 = Ex.

# 4  Squats

From standing, 'sit' down as if to touch the seat of an
imaginary chair and stand again.
Target in 30 seconds: 20 = F, 25 = G, 30 = Ex.

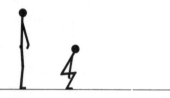

# 5  Squat jumps

As squats, above, but instead of standing up from the squat
position *jump into the air with full extension of the body.*
In this exercise it is also usual to crouch down a little lower
in the squat, so as to touch the floor with the hands.
Target in 30 seconds: 15 = F, 20 = G, 25 = Ex.

# 6  Burpees

These are a combination of squat thrusts and squat jumps
– a squat thrust is followed by a squat jump.
Target in 30 seconds: 12 = F, 16 = G, 20 = Ex.
(see diagram, page 111.)

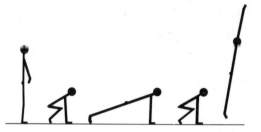

## 7 Step ups

(a) On to a *solid* chair, step up steadily, alternating legs (do not always lead with the same leg). Both feet should be placed on the chair.
Target in 30 seconds: 20 = F, 25 = G, 30 = Ex.

(b) On to a bench, preferably held steady, step up rapidly, again alternating the lead leg.
Target in 30 seconds: 30 = F, 40 = G, 55 = Ex.

## 8 Dips

Use parallel bars, or bars across a cave unit, approximately shoulder width apart. Start with arms straight, supporting the body weight, and then lower the body by bending the elbows to 90°, then straighten. This is a very demanding exercise.
Maximum targets: 3 = F, 5 = G, 8 = Ex.

## 9 Chins or pull ups using the bar

(a) For beginners, have the bar at approximately 30 centimetres above head height. Grasp the bar and jump up to raise the chin above the bar. Lower the body to the ground and jump again (that is, the pull up is assisted by a jump).
Target in 30 seconds: 20 = F, 25 = G, 30 = Ex.

(b) With the bar approximately 50 centimetres above head height, hang from it, feet clear of the ground, and pull up until the chin is above the bar; lower and repeat, keeping the feet off the ground. The arms must be straightened each time.
Maximum targets: 5 = F, 8 = G, 10 = Ex.

NOTE – for (a) and (b), a bench, chair, or stool can be used to allow different sized children to use the same bar. For (b), the grasp of the bar may be either under-grasp (with palms and finger tips towards the child) or overgrasp (with palms and finger tips away from the child). The undergrasp is slightly easier.

This list is by no means definitive, but provides a sample of the basic exercises.

# PARTNER ACTIVITIES

A few activities involving partners can increase general strength and the ability to handle body weight.

## 1  Tug of war

(a)  Face a partner and grasp right hand to right wrist. The object is to pull the partner over a line (drawn either behind each partner or between them). The pull must be steady, not jerking.

(b)  As above, but partners grasp both hands.

(c)  As above, but partners link elbows.

(d)  Groups of 4 to 6 link by grasping hand to wrist to form a circle round a skittle. The object is to pull one person over the skittle.

## 2  Chinese boxing

Grasp the partner's right wrist with the left hand. The object is to touch the partner with the right hand, so each partner is pushing with the right hand and resisting with the left.

## 3  Stubborn donkey

Grasp the back of a partner's head with linked hands. Attempt to pull the 'stubborn donkey' forwards while the donkey resists. The donkey must keep his/her head up and not slip the grasp by lowering the head.

## 4  Pushing contest

(a) Push with hands on partner's shoulders, either standing or crouching.
(b) Push shoulder to shoulder, head to the left of the partner's head, as in a rugby scrum.

The above activities are best covered in short, sharp bursts rather than in prolonged sessions. Again, they are by no means definitive, but should serve as ideas for other activities.

# Appendix II
## Suggested Links with Classroom Activities

*Language and reading*
Stories of great races or competitions (for example, 'The First Four Minutes' by Roger Bannister).
Poems, such as 'If' by Rudyard Kipling; 'The Sprinters' by Leem Murchison; 'Song of the Ungirt Runners' by Charles Hamilton Sorley.

*Poetry writing*
The feelings of running, jumping and throwing. Excitement and nerves during competition, and pleasure or disappointment at the result. Sports Day – noises, activities.

*Factual writing*
Reports on Sports Day and other competitions. Description of events and rules for competition.

*Creative writing*
Set at the Olympics or some other major event.

*Speaking/listening*
Discussions on the organisation of Sports Day (children can often offer valuable insight). Tape-recording of real or imaginary competitions, and 'interviews' with stars as if for radio or T.V. Debates on controversial subjects, such as 'shamateurism', or political interference on sport (for example, 1980 Olympics – should G.B. have sent a team, or competition with or in South Africa). These are delicate areas and teachers must sit on the fence and present both sides of the argument.

*Topic work*
1 *History of the Olympics* (both Ancient and Modern), which can also provide an insight into world or European history of the time (cancellations due to war, problems related to the depression, exclusion of countries, and so on). For much older children the build-up to the 1936 Olympics makes an absorbing study.

2 *Olympic/European/World/Commonwealth* championships and European and World Cup competitions can provide many ideas.

(a) Select certain countries and locate them, study their population, their climate, their way of life and so on, and compare and contrast them.

(b) Contrast British records or one season's best with Olympic or World records. Actually measure some distances. The children will be staggered at the length of an 8.90 metre long jump or 90 metre javelin throw.

(c) Follow the fortunes of certain British stars as they tour Europe competing in numerous spectaculars. Look up air/train/road routes.

3 *Science*

Diet and health. The effects of exercise on the heart beat, the need for calories, vitamins, protein and carbohydrates. Contrast physical jobs with sedentary ones in their needs.

The use of muscle groups in running, jumping, throwing. Limbs as levers. The effect of fatigue on co-ordination, speed and strength. NOTE *Sports and Games*, from the series SCIENCE IN A TOPIC by D. Kincaid and P.S. Coles (Hulton), contains many useful suggestions.

4 *Mathematics*

Utilise the wealth of statistics available from the testing and measuring to:

(a) total points/times/distances for team competitions;

(b) produce bar charts by class/group related to events or points or incentive scheme awards – pie charts and pictograms are also possible;

(c) work out modes/means/medians.

The practical mathematics involved is timing, measuring and accurate recording.

Scale plans can show athletics areas, from a simple scale plan of a netball court showing the layout of the various activities through to a full track layout to test the most able.

5 *R.E./Moral Education*

Athletics as part of ancient religious festivals. Cheating, codes of conduct, ethics, need for rules and so on.

6 *Music*

Theme music from television and films ('Chariots of Fire').

The above suggestions are by no means exhaustive, and as ideas are pursued so fresh ideas will occur.

# Index